Real English in American Culture

BIG POT

BIG POT ②

Author Jack McBain
Publisher Chung Kyudo
Editors Kwon Minjeong, Cho Sangik
Designers Jeong Hyunseok, Lee Seunghyun
Photo Credit www.shutterstock.com

First Published in September 2020
By Darakwon, Inc.
Darakwon Bldg., 211, Munbal-ro, Paju-si, Gyeonggi-do 10881
Republic of Korea
Tel: 82-2-736-2031 (Ext. 552)

Price ₩15,000
ISBN 978-89-277-0983-1 14740
     978-89-277-0981-7 14740 (set)

www.darakwon.co.kr

Main Book / Free MP3 Available Online
7 6 5 4 3 2 1   20 21 22 23 24

Real English in American Culture

BIG POT

Jack McBain

 DARAKWON

Contents

To the Students ·· 6

Structure of the Book ·· 7

Plan of the Book ··· 8

Unit **01** Fashion and Style ··· 10

Unit **02** Sports Nuts ·· 20

Unit **03** Americans and Their Cars ·································· 30

Unit **04** Guns in America ·· 40

Unit **05** Dating ··· 50

Unit **06** Travel in America ··· 60

Unit **07** Health Care ·· 70

Unit **08** At the Hair Salon ·· 80

Unit **09** Professional Life ··· 90

Unit **10** Weddings ··· 100

Unit **11** Finding a Home ·· 110

Unit **12** Spaces for Everyone ······································· 120

Answer Key ·· 130

To the Students

BIG POT is a two-level series for adult and young adult English language learners. This dynamic series contains material appropriate for students ranging from a beginner level to an intermediate level. It is designed to provide students with basic background knowledge about American culture and to help them learn English expressions related to it. Each book in the series provides interesting, thought-provoking material in order to meet the linguistic needs of a diverse community of language learners.

BIG POT 2 has twelve units, each of which consists of a warm-up, three supporting lessons, a wrap-up, and a reading. The book covers numerous aspects of American culture through stimulating conversations. Each conversation provides the context for supplementary grammar, language point, and speaking activities. Students will find topics such as fashion, sports, cars & driving, and traveling interesting and relevant to living, studying, and working abroad. By practicing conversations related to life in the United States, students will gain a better understanding of the cultural nuances which exist in the large cultural landscape which is America.

As a multi-skill course book, *BIG POT* introduces essential linguistic and cultural information to students. Students will have the opportunity to read about American culture, practice contextually accurate dialogues with one another, answer interesting grammar and language point questions, and finally, participate in a variety of interesting speaking activities with partners and small groups. The purpose of this book is to provide context to the language, a context which will give students access and insight into how Americans actually use the language in everyday life.

Jack McBain

Author's Acknowledgments

The author would like to express his utmost gratitude to the editor Minjeong Kwon. Without her tireless work and guidance, this project would not have been possible. He would also like to acknowledge the contributions of Darakwon management and the graphic design team. Finally, he would like to extend a heartfelt thanks to his family, who has been incredibly patient during the writing process.

Structure of the Book

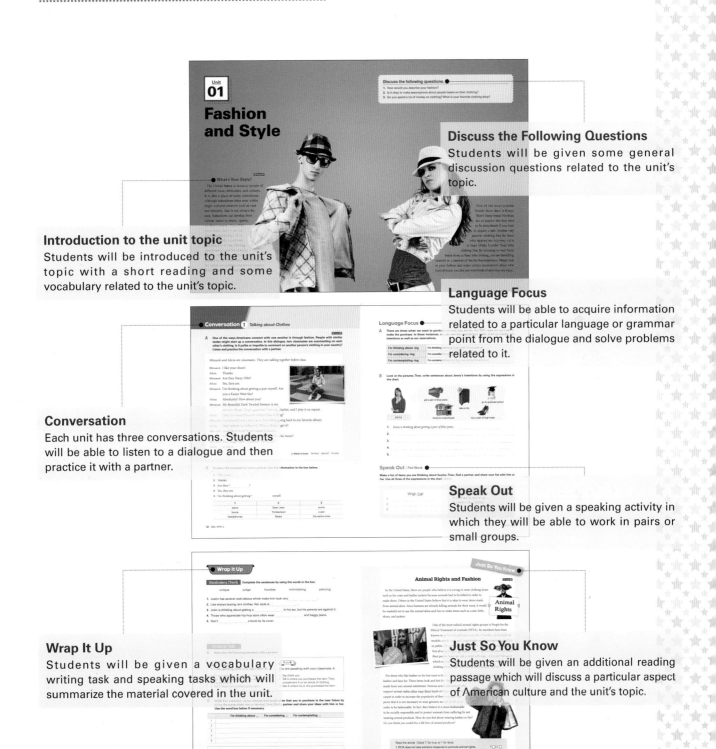

Discuss the Following Questions
Students will be given some general discussion questions related to the unit's topic.

Introduction to the unit topic
Students will be introduced to the unit's topic with a short reading and some vocabulary related to the unit's topic.

Language Focus
Students will be able to acquire information related to a particular language or grammar point from the dialogue and solve problems related to it.

Conversation
Each unit has three conversations. Students will be able to listen to a dialogue and then practice it with a partner.

Speak Out
Students will be given a speaking activity in which they will be able to work in pairs or small groups.

Wrap It Up
Students will be given a vocabulary writing task and speaking tasks which will summarize the material covered in the unit.

Just So You Know
Students will be given an additional reading passage which will discuss a particular aspect of American culture and the unit's topic.

Plan of the Book

Unit	Title	Topic	Conversation
01	**Fashion and Style**	Fashion & Body Art	- Talking about Clothes - You Can't Judge a Book by Its Cover - Talking about Piercings
02	**Sports Nuts**	Sports	- A Super Bowl Party - At a Baseball Game - A Pick-up Game
03	**Americans and Their Cars**	Cars & Driving	- At the DMV - Learning to Drive - Buying a Used Car
04	**Guns in America**	Guns	- Talking about Hunting - An Open-carry State - First-person Shooter Games
05	**Dating**	Dating	- Are You Flirting with Me? - Asking Someone Out on a Date - Using Dating Apps
06	**Travel in America**	Traveling	- A Day Trip - A Weekend Getaway - Spring Break
07	**Health Care**	Health	- Healthcare Providers - Making a Doctor's Appointment - Visiting the ER
08	**At the Hair Salon**	Hair & Beauty	- Making an Appointment with My Hairdresser - Walk-ins - At the Beauty Salon
09	**Professional Life**	Work & Jobs	- A Job Interview - Office Etiquette - Giving Two Weeks' Notice
10	**Weddings**	Weddings & Marriage	- An Invitation to Be a Maid of Honor - Searching a Wedding Registry - A Wedding DJ
11	**Finding a Home**	Housing	- Viewing a House - Searching for an Apartment - Signing a Lease
12	**Spaces for Everyone**	Public Spaces	- Borrowing a Book from the Library - Hiking in Yosemite - A Summer Block Party

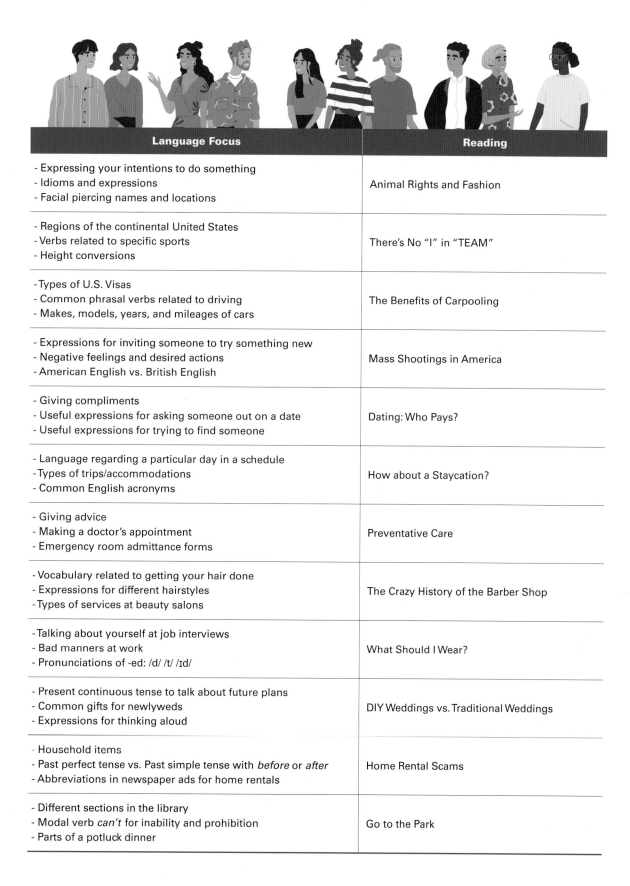

Language Focus	Reading
- Expressing your intentions to do something - Idioms and expressions - Facial piercing names and locations	Animal Rights and Fashion
- Regions of the continental United States - Verbs related to specific sports - Height conversions	There's No "I" in "TEAM"
- Types of U.S. Visas - Common phrasal verbs related to driving - Makes, models, years, and mileages of cars	The Benefits of Carpooling
- Expressions for inviting someone to try something new - Negative feelings and desired actions - American English vs. British English	Mass Shootings in America
- Giving compliments - Useful expressions for asking someone out on a date - Useful expressions for trying to find someone	Dating: Who Pays?
- Language regarding a particular day in a schedule - Types of trips/accommodations - Common English acronyms	How about a Staycation?
- Giving advice - Making a doctor's appointment - Emergency room admittance forms	Preventative Care
- Vocabulary related to getting your hair done - Expressions for different hairstyles - Types of services at beauty salons	The Crazy History of the Barber Shop
- Talking about yourself at job interviews - Bad manners at work - Pronunciations of -ed: /d/ /t/ /ɪd/	What Should I Wear?
- Present continuous tense to talk about future plans - Common gifts for newlyweds - Expressions for thinking aloud	DIY Weddings vs. Traditional Weddings
- Household items - Past perfect tense vs. Past simple tense with *before* or *after* - Abbreviations in newspaper ads for home rentals	Home Rental Scams
- Different sections in the library - Modal verb *can't* for inability and prohibition - Parts of a potluck dinner	Go to the Park

Unit 01

Fashion and Style

◎Track 01

What's Your Style?

The United States is home to people of different races, ethnicities, and cultures. It is also a place of many subcultures. Although subcultures often exist within larger cultural contexts such as race and ethnicity, that is not always the case. Subcultures can develop from similar tastes in music, sports, and other interests. One of the prominent ways you can show membership in, or affiliation with, a particular subculture is by the clothing you choose to wear. For example, hip-hop fashion is a billion-dollar industry in the United States. Several rappers and artists sell clothing related to the hip-hop industry through their various clothing lines.

Discuss the following questions.

1. How would you describe your fashion?
2. Is it okay to make assumptions about people based on their clothing?
3. Do you spend a lot of money on clothing? What is your favorite clothing shop?

One of the most popular brands these days is Kanye West's Yeezy brand. His shoes are so popular that they have to be preordered if you want to acquire a pair. Another very popular clothing line for those who appreciate hip-hop style is Sean Diddy Combs' Sean John clothing line. By choosing to wear Yeezy brand shoes or Sean John clothing, you are identifying yourself as a member of the hip-hop subculture. People look at your fashion and make certain assumptions about what kind of music you like and what kinds of activities you enjoy.

Conversation ❶ *Talking about Clothes*

Track 02

A One of the ways Americans connect with one another is through fashion. People with similar tastes might start up a conversation. In this dialogue, two classmates are commenting on each other's clothing. Is it polite or impolite to comment on another person's clothing in your country? Listen and practice the conversation with a partner.

Minseok and Alicia are classmates. They are talking together before class.

Minseok	I like your shoes!
Alicia	Thanks.
Minseok	Are they Yeezy 350s?
Alicia	Yes, they are.
Minseok	I'm thinking about getting a pair myself. Are you a Kanye West fan?
Alicia	Absolutely! How about you?
Minseok	*My Beautiful Dark Twisted Fantasy* is my favorite album. It's programmed into my playlist, and I play it on repeat.
Alicia	Have you heard his new album *Jesus Is King*?
Minseok	I've listened to it a few times, but I keep going back to my favorite album.
Alicia	Your hoodie is really cool. Where did you get it?
Minseok	I bought it in my home country, Korea.
Alicia	What does that hand gesture on your hoodie mean?
Minseok	It's a finger heart. It means "I love you."
Alicia	I love it.

⊘ **Words to Know**   fantasy   playlist   hoodie

B Practice the conversation with a partner. Use the information in the box below.

A I like your ¹ _____ !

B Thanks.

A Are they ² _____ ?

B Yes, they are.

A I'm thinking about getting ³ _____ myself.

1	2	3
jeans	Sean Jean	some
boots	Timberland	a pair
headphones	Beats	the same ones

Language Focus

A There are times when we want to purchase an item, but we are not 100% sure we are ready to make the purchase. In these instances, we can use the expressions in the chart to express our intentions as well as our reservations.

I'm thinking about -ing	I'm thinking about getting a pair of sunglasses.
I'm considering -ing	I'm considering taking the next semester off.
I'm contemplating -ing	I'm contemplating traveling abroad for the summer.

B Look at the pictures. Then, write sentences about Jenny's intentions by using the expressions in the chart.

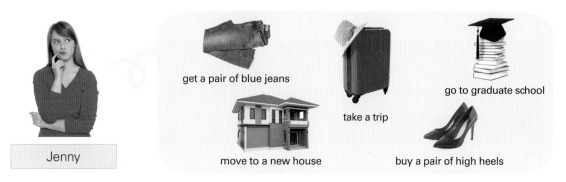

Jenny

get a pair of blue jeans

move to a new house

take a trip

go to graduate school

buy a pair of high heels

1. *Jenny is thinking about getting a pair of blue jeans.*

2. _____

3. _____

4. _____

5. _____

Speak Out | Pair Work

Make a list of items you are thinking about buying. Then, find a partner and share your list with him or her. Use all three of the expressions in the chart above.

Wish List

1 _____

2 _____

3 _____

I'm thinking about buying a pair of Apple Airpods.
I'm considering purchasing ...
I'm contemplating getting ...

Conversation ❷ *You Can't Judge a Book by Its Cover*

Track 03

A People choose all kinds of looks in order to be fashionable. Some of them are mainstream, and some are not. We tend to make assumptions about those whose fashion is outside of the mainstream, and sometimes those assumptions are wrong. Here is a dialogue between two people about their neighbor. Listen and practice the conversation with a partner.

Shinzo and Zara are talking about their neighbor, Justin.

Shinzo   Have you seen the guy in apartment 202?

Zara   Yeah. That's Justin's apartment.

Shinzo   You know him? Doesn't he scare you?

Zara   Not at all. Justin's a great guy.

Shinzo   What about the tattoos? He even has some on his neck.

Zara   You can't judge a book by its cover, Shinzo.

Shinzo   What do you mean by that?

Zara   Justin might look intimidating on the outside, but he's a big teddy bear on the inside. You should introduce yourself to him. I promise you that he's nice.

Shinzo   He said hello to me the other day, but I couldn't even respond.

Zara   You should have said hello. He loves talking to people from other countries. He travels quite a bit.

Shinzo   Really?

Zara   Yeah, and he's funny, too. He's a tattoo artist, so that's why he has so many tattoos.

Shinzo   I see. I shouldn't have judged him so quickly. I'll say hello to him the next time I see him.

⊘ **Words to Know**   tattoo   judge   intimidating

B Practice the conversation with a partner. Use the information in the box below.

A   Have you seen the ¹ _____ in apartment 202?

B   Yeah. That's ² _____ apartment.

A   Doesn't ³ _____ scare you?

B   Not at all.

A   What about the ⁴ _____ ?

B   You can't judge a book by its cover.

1	2	3	4
woman	Elaine's	she	tongue piercing
man	Chen's	he	nose piercing
guy	Brian's	he	shaved head

Language Focus

A Native English speakers tend to use idioms and expressions that non-native English speakers might not understand. Here are some examples of very common idioms and expressions in English. Try to match the idioms and expressions with their correct meanings.

Idioms and Expressions		
a. *You can't judge a book by its cover.*		to reveal a secret
b. *see eye to eye*		sick or depressed
c. *under the weather*		to share the same opinion about something
d. *the best of both worlds*		something that is easy and simple to do
e. *a piece of cake*		the benefits of two opportunities simultaneously
f. *let the cat out of the bag*	*a*	not to prejudge someone before speaking with him or her

B Complete the sentences by using the idioms and expressions from the chart.

1. I can't believe Beth _____ .
She wasn't supposed to tell anyone about the party.

2. Sarah can't attend class today because she feels _____ .

3. My wife and I _____ on saving money.

4. Maria thought the English test she took today was _____ .

5. It looks like the game will end by six, so I can go to Joe's party, too. I get _____ !

6. Alexis has tattoos all over her body, but _____ .
She's really friendly.

Speak Out

A **Pair Work** Discuss the questions about idioms and expressions with a partner.

1. Which English idioms and expressions have you found to be the most difficult to understand? Why?

2. Do you think it is important to learn English idioms and expressions? Why?

B **Class Activity** Translate two idioms from your own language into English. Then, read them aloud to the class. See if students who do not speak your native language can guess the meanings of the idioms.

	Your Own Language	English
1		
2		

Conversation ③ *Talking about Piercings*

Track 04

A Similar to tattoos, piercings are another popular form of body art for Americans. It is not uncommon these days to see eyebrow piercings, nostril and septum piercings of the nose, and ear piercings of the lobes and the cartilage. Are piercings popular in your country? Listen and practice the conversation with a partner.

Dongmin is drinking coffee and talking with his girlfriend, Kylie.

Dongmin Can I ask you something?

Kylie You can ask me anything.

Dongmin Which piercing hurt more: the tongue piercing or the nose piercing?

Kylie The nose piercing hurt more because it wasn't in a typical location.

Dongmin What do you mean?

Kylie Instead of having my nostril pierced, I had my septum pierced.

Dongmin Your septum?

Kylie Yeah. It separates the nostrils, and it's kind of thick, so it hurts a lot when someone sticks a needle through it.

Dongmin Why do you like piercings so much?

Kylie I don't know. I got my tongue pierced when I was eighteen. After that, I kept adding more piercings. Don't you like them?

Dongmin I do. I think they look really cool. I'm just wondering whether your piercings will make it difficult for you to find a job.

Kylie Not in my line of work. I want to be a hairdresser, and salons encourage their hairdressers to be unique.

⊘ **Words to Know** piercing typical separate unique

B Practice the conversation with a partner. Use the information in the box below.

A Can I ask you something?

B ¹ ....

A Which piercing hurt more: the nose piercing or the ² .... piercing?

B The nose piercing ³ .... because it wasn't in a typical location.

1	2	3
Of course.	tongue	killed
Sure. What is it?	eyebrow	was torture
Shoot.	lip	was agonizing

Language Focus

A   These days, there are a lot of places on the face where young people get piercings. Look at the names of places for piercings.

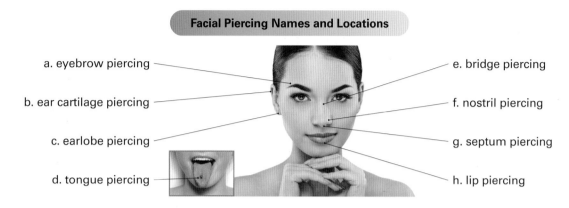

Facial Piercing Names and Locations

a. eyebrow piercing

b. ear cartilage piercing

c. earlobe piercing

d. tongue piercing

e. bridge piercing

f. nostril piercing

g. septum piercing

h. lip piercing

B   Match the names of the piercings with the correct pictures.

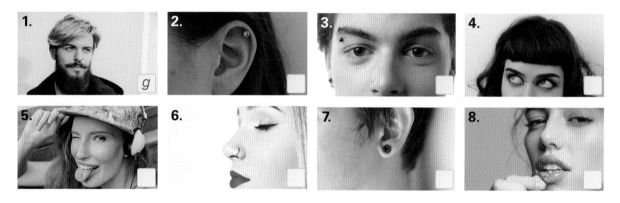

Speak Out | Pair Work

Find a partner. Then, imagine you are at a tattoo and piercing parlor, and you want to get some piercings on your face. By using the piercing names above, tell your partner where you want your piercings. Let your partner draw your piercings on the faces below.

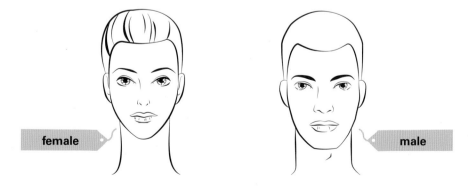

female

male

I would like my right eyebrow, my lip, and both of my earlobes pierced.

Wrap It Up

Vocabulary Check Complete the sentences by using the words in the box.

unique	judge	hoodies	intimidating	piercing

1. Justin has several neck tattoos which make him look very _____ .
2. Lisa enjoys buying rare clothes. Her style is _____ .
3. John is thinking about getting a _____ in his ear, but his parents are against it.
4. Those who appreciate hip-hop style often wear _____ and baggy jeans.
5. Don't _____ a book by its cover.

Situation Talk

A Role-play the following situation with a partner.

Role **A**	Role **B**
You are speaking with your classmate, B.	*You are speaking with your classmate, A.*
1. Compliment B on an article of clothing. 2. Ask B where he or she purchased the item. 3. Say thank you. 4. Tell B where you purchased the item.	1. Say thank you. 2. Tell A where you purchased the item. Then, compliment A on an article of clothing. 3. Ask A where he or she purchased the item.

B Write five sentences about clothes and accessories that you intend to purchase in the near future by using the expressions you've learned. Then, find a partner and share your ideas with him or her. Use the word box below if necessary.

	I'm thinking about … I'm considering … I'm contemplating …
1	
2	
3	
4	
5	

cardigan	hoodie	sweatshirt	leather jacket	trench coat	tracksuit
jumpsuit	cargo pants	miniskirt	swimsuit	rash guard	sunglasses
beanie	handbag	briefcase	running shoes	sandals	hiking boots

Animal Rights and Fashion

🔊 Track 05

In the United States, there are people who believe it is wrong to wear clothing items such as fur coats and leather jackets because animals had to be killed in order to make them. Others in the United States believe that it is okay to wear items made from animal skins. Since humans are already killing animals for their meat, it would be wasteful not to use the animal skins and furs to make items such as coats, belts, shoes, and jackets.

One of the most radical animal rights groups is People for the Ethical Treatment of Animals (PETA). Its members have been known to go to such extremes as to throw buckets of red paint on models, movie stars, and singers who were wearing leather and fur in public. The red paint is supposed to signify an animal's blood. Not all animal rights groups go to such extreme measures to make their points. Some groups protest with signs or pay for billboards which ask onlookers to reconsider their positions when choosing clothing items made from actual animal skins and furs.

For those who like leather or fur but want to be socially responsible, there are options such as faux leather and faux fur. These items look and feel like the genuine material but are made from non-animal substitutes. Famous actors and singers who support animal rights often wear these kinds of items on the red carpet in order to increase the popularity of these products and prove that it is not necessary to wear genuine animal products in order to be fashionable. In fact, they believe it is more fashionable to be socially responsible and to protect animals from suffering by not wearing animal products. How do you feel about wearing leather or fur? Do you think you could live a life free of animal products?

Read the article. Check T for true or F for false.

1. PETA does not take extreme measures to promote animal rights.   T ☐ / F ☐
2. Some famous people have had red paint thrown on them by PETA activists.   T ☐ / F ☐
3. Faux fur and faux leather contain a small amount of animal products.   T ☐ / F ☐

Unit 02

Sports Nuts

🔊 Track 06

Professional Sports in America

Americans are crazy about sports. The country's passion and excitement for the National Football League (NFL), the National Basketball Association (NBA), and Major League Baseball (MLB) know no bounds. In the United States, it is very common for people to regularly attend professional sporting events at large stadiums in the biggest cities across the nation.

While some cities and states have no professional teams, others have several. Some even have multiple teams for the same sport. California, for example, has four NBA teams: the Sacramento Kings, the Golden State Warriors, the Los Angeles Clippers, and the Los Angeles Lakers. Los Angeles is such a large city that it has two NBA teams!

It is hard to say which professional sport is the most popular in the U.S. because there are so many fans of multiple sports, but it is probably safe to say that American football is enjoyed by the widest array of fans. The Super Bowl, the name of the championship game, is one of the largest television events of the year. 30-second commercial spots during the Super Bowl cost more than five million dollars. Worldwide, soccer is the most popular sport; however, in the United States, it does not approach the popularity of the NFL, the NBA, and MLB.

Discuss the following questions.

1. Do you enjoy watching sports on television? If yes, which ones?
2. Do you play any sports now? If not, have you ever played sports? Which ones?
3. Are people from your country crazy about sports? If yes, which ones?

Conversation ① A Super Bowl Party

⊘ Track 07

A If you live in the U.S. for an entire year, you will get to experience the Super Bowl. If you are really lucky, one of your friends will throw a Super Bowl party. At Super Bowl parties, you will find beer and soda as well as potato chips, buffalo wings, nachos, pizza, and other delicious but unhealthy foods. This is a conversation between two guests at a party. Is there a popular yearly sporting event in your country? Listen and practice the conversation with a partner.

Tess and Pedro are chatting at a Super Bowl party.

Tess Who are you cheering for, Pedro?

Pedro I don't know. I'm not that familiar with American football.

Tess I'm a Patriots fan. I grew up in New England, so all of my family members are huge Pats fans as well.

Pedro I guess I'll cheer for the Pats, too, then.

Tess Cool. Is this your first Super Bowl party?

Pedro Yes, it is. There's so much food.

Tess I know. Todd and Rebecca always throw the biggest Super Bowl parties with the best spreads. Have you tried Rebecca's homemade wings or Todd's barbecue ribs?

Pedro I tried both of them, but I can't decide which was better because they were both so …

Tess *(interrupting)* Oh, the Patriots just scored a field goal. Hooray! Go Pats!

Pedro Go Pats! What's the score now?

Tess It's the 3rd quarter, and the game is tied. I know they can win this!

Pedro Go Pats!

⊘ **Words to Know** chat cheer for spread tie

B Practice the conversation with a partner. Use the information in the box below.

A Who are you cheering for?

B I don't know. I'm not that familiar with ¹ _____ .

A I grew up in ² _____ , so I'm a huge ³ _____ fan.

B ⁴ _____ I'll cheer for them, too.

1	2	3	4
the NBA	Los Angeles	Lakers	In that case,
baseball	New England	Red Sox	Well, then
American football	Wisconsin	Packers	I guess

Language Focus

A   Although the United States is a country comprised of fifty individual states, there are larger regional names which Americans use in casual conversation. Look at the map below.

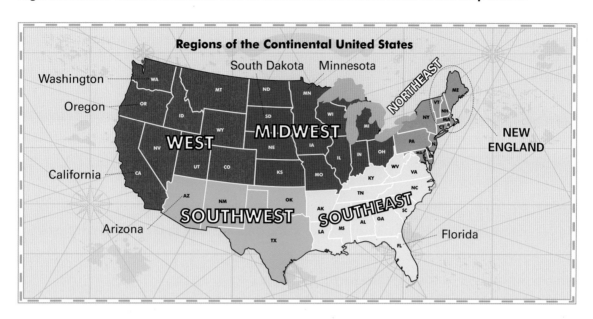

B   Read the dialogues and complete the sentences with the correct regional names.

1. A   Where are you from?

    B   I'm from Minnesota.

    A   I'm from the _____, too. I'm from South Dakota.

2. A   Have you ever been to the _____?

    B   Once. I visited a friend in Arizona.

3. A   I'm planning to travel through the _____ this year.

    B   Oh, it's a great place to visit. I've been to California, Oregon, and Washington.

4. A   I'm a big fan of the football team the New England Patriots.

    B   Did you grow up in the _____?

    A   Yes, I did.

5. A   I've never been to the _____ of the Unites States.

    B   Really? It's very nice. You must go to the beautiful beaches in Florida.

Speak Out | Pair Work

Find a partner. Then, tell your partner which region in the United States you would like to visit and why. Include which individual states in the region most interest you and why you like them.

Conversation ❷ *At a Baseball Game*

⊙ Track 08

A Many Americans enjoy attending live professional sporting events. Just like sporting events in other countries, the closer your seat is to the action on the court or field, the more expensive the tickets are. The cheap seats at baseball games can be purchased for approximately $20 to $25 per ticket. How much are the cheap seats in your country? Listen and practice the conversation with a partner.

Gino is inviting Hayoung to a professional baseball game.

Hayoung *(phone ringing)* Hello.

Gino Hey, Hayoung. This is Gino from English class.

Hayoung Hi, Gino, What's up?

Gino I have some free tickets to a baseball game on Thursday, and I was wondering if you'd like to go with me.

Hayoung Sure. I love baseball. Who's playing?

Gino The L.A. Dodgers are playing the Chicago Cubs. Clayton Kershaw is pitching.

Hayoung Great. I love him. Where are we sitting?

Gino Unfortunately, our seats are in the nosebleed section.

Hayoung The nosebleed section? What does that mean?

Gino They're high up in the stands—the cheap seats.

Hayoung That's okay. I just love the atmosphere in the stadium.

Gino Me, too. I love the smell of hot dogs and beer!
Do you go to baseball games in Korea?

Hayoung I sure do. I've been to lots of games back home.

Gino Great. I'll pick you up at six o'clock on Thursday.

⊘ **Words to Know**   pitch   nosebleed section   stands   stadium

B Practice the conversation with a partner. Use the information in the box below.

A I have some free tickets to a ¹ _____ game, and I was wondering if you'd like to go with me.

B ² _____ . Where are we sitting?

A Our seats are ³ _____ .

B Great. It sounds like fun.

1	2	3
basketball	I'd like that	courtside
baseball	Definitely	right behind home plate
football	Absolutely	three rows up at the 50-yard line

Language Focus

A   In English, we have different names for the kinds of surfaces sports are played on. For example, basketball is played on a court whereas soccer is played on a field. A court is a hard, flat surface whereas a field is a soft, grassy surface. Look at the chart and learn some verbs related to sports that are played on a field and a court.

Field	Court	Verbs Related to Specific Sports	
soccer	basketball	**throw** the ball	**catch** the ball
baseball	volleyball	**hit** the ball	**kick** the ball
football	tennis	**spike** the ball	**toss** the ball
softball	badminton	**shoot** the ball	**pass** the ball
lacrosse	racquetball	**dunk** the ball	**dribble** the ball

B   Complete the sentences with the correct verbs from the box below.

1. Lebron James _____ the ball down the court and dunked the ball.

2. Nadal moved quickly on the court and _____ the tennis ball past his opponent.

3. Tom Brady _____ the football down the field to the receiver, who scored a touchdown.

4. Messi _____ the ball into the net and celebrated by running across the field.

5. Yeongyung Kim _____ the ball onto the opponent's court and scored a point for her team.

6. The center fielder dove for the ball and _____ it.

threw	kicked	dribbled	spiked	hit	caught

Speak Out | Class Activity

Have your teacher conduct a classroom survey by asking students to raise their hands when the teacher mentions their favorite sport. Then, discuss the questions below.

	basketball	baseball	football	soccer	other
Number of students whose favorite sport is …					

1. Which sport was the most popular in your class? Why do you think it was the most popular?

2. If you chose "other," what is your favorite sport? Share your answer with the class.

3. Is there anyone in your class who does not like sports? If so, why not?

Conversation ③ *A Pick-up Game*

Track 09

A   **Pick-up games are very popular in the United States. They are a great way to make friends with people who have similar interests as you. There are plenty of public basketball courts, tennis courts, and soccer fields for people to get together during the week or on weekends to play games together. Do you play in any pick-up games in your country? Listen and practice the conversation with a partner.**

Mark and Jeonghyun are talking about organizing a pick-up basketball game.

Mark	Do you play basketball, Jeonghyun?
Jeonghyun	I sure do. I play constantly back home.
Mark	What position do you play?
Jeonghyun	I'm a pretty good guard. I can dribble, shoot 3s, and pass the ball well.
Mark	We have a pick-up game every Saturday on the campus basketball courts. Would you like to come?
Jeonghyun	Of course.
Mark	Why don't you meet me at the courts at three o'clock on Saturday? We'll shoot around a little bit before the game.
Jeonghyun	Sounds great. My roommate plays basketball, too. He's good.
Mark	How tall is he?
Jeonghyun	He's 6' 6". He's an excellent center. *6' 6" = 6 feet 6 inches
Mark	No way! Can he dunk?
Jeonghyun	Absolutely.
Mark	Bring him along, too. Together, we'll be unstoppable.

⊘ **Words to Know**   constantly   position   guard   center

B   **Practice the conversation with a partner. Use the information in the box below.**

A How tall is he?

B He's ¹ _____ . He's an excellent ² _____ .

A Can he ³ _____ ?

B Absolutely.

1	2	3
5' 7"	point guard	shoot well
6' 2"	forward	jump high
6' 8"	center	block shots

Language Focus

A In the United States, the standard units for measuring a person's height are feet and inches. This is different than the global metric standard of meters and centimeters. Look at the chart.

Height Conversions
1 inch = 2.54 centimeters
1 foot = 0.3048 meters
1 yard = 0.9144 meters
1 mile = 1.6093 kilometers
1 centimeter = 0.3937 inches
1 meter = 3.2808 feet
1 kilometer = 0.6214 miles

*1 foot = 12 inches

6 feet 8 inches or six foot eight

6' 8" = 204cm

2 meters 4 centimeters

B Read the dialogues and make conversions based on the chart above.

1. A How tall are you, Jiwoo?

　B I'm 172 centimeters tall.

➡ Jiwoo is _____ feet _____ inches tall.

2. A How far is your house from here, Byunghun?

　B It's about ten kilometers.

➡ Byunghun's house is _____ miles from here.

3. A How long is an American football field?

　B It's 100 yards.

➡ An American football field is _____ meters long.

4. A How tall is Charles? He's a giant!

　B I think he's two meters and nineteen centimeters tall.

➡ Charles is _____ feet _____ inches tall.

Speak Out | Pair Work

Ask three students how tall they are in meters and centimeters. Then, do a conversion and tell them how tall they are in feet and inches.

A *How tall are you?*
B *I'm 173 centimeters tall.*
A *You are five feet eight inches tall. / You are five foot eight.*

Wrap It Up

Vocabulary Check — Match the words with their correct definitions.

1. tie •
2. stands •
3. constantly •
4. chat •
5. pitch •

• ⓐ to have a casual conversation
• ⓑ all the time or regularly
• ⓒ to have the same score in a competition or game
• ⓓ to throw the ball to a batter in the game of baseball
• ⓔ a section where people sit or stand to watch a game or event

Situation Talk

A   Role-play the following situation with a partner.

You are watching the Super Bowl at a Super Bowl party.

1. Ask B which team he or she is cheering for.
2. Tell B that you are cheering for your favorite team, the New York Giants.
3. Tell B that the Giants are playing the New England Patriots. Tell B that the Patriots are the Giants' biggest rival.
4. Tell B that the Giants have 7 and the Patriots have 0, but it is only the first quarter. Ask B if he or she has tried Richard's famous nachos yet.
5. Tell B that he or she must try the nachos. Tell B that they're the best you've ever had.

You are watching your first Super Bowl at your friend's Super Bowl party.

1. Tell A you do not know much about football. Tell A you do not have a favorite team.
2. Tell A that you will cheer for the Giants, too. Ask A who the Giants are playing.
3. Ask A what the score is.
4. Tell A that you haven't tried them yet, but you will.

B   Answer the "Would you rather...?" questions with a partner.

1. Would you rather watch an American football game or a soccer game?
2. Would you rather sit in the nosebleed section at a soccer game or behind home plate at a Major League Baseball game?
3. Would you rather be a good NBA player or a great racquetball player?
4. Would you rather play but always lose or sit on the bench but always win?
5. Would you rather spend the day with your favorite athlete or your favorite movie star?

There's No "I" in "TEAM"

🔊 Track 10

Americans are often thought of as selfish and individualistic. Although there are aspects of American culture which focus on personal advancement and self-fulfillment, there is a long history of Americans working together in order to accomplish difficult tasks. The West was not settled individually but by organized groups of trailblazers who created the first inroads to the harsh, unforgiving wilderness. Masses of young American men volunteered to fight during World War II, many of them losing their lives in the European and Pacific theaters.

Teamwork is so important to Americans that team sports organizations were created so that children could learn how to work together at young ages. There is Little League for young baseball players and Pop Warner football for young football players. Soccer is also very popular with children. Team sports are so important that many universities look positively on participation in team sports when reviewing college entrance applications.

Team sports are not only for the players, but they are also for the fans. University students often attend their universities' football, basketball, and hockey games to cheer for their schools. Team spirit spreads across campuses, infecting everyone with cheer. Not only do team sports teach young people how to work together and win, but they also teach them how not to be sore losers. When each member of the team contributes his or her most to the game, the team can be satisfied knowing that they played as well as they could, and they did it together. The saying, "There is no I in TEAM," could not be truer today than when the phrase was first coined years ago.

Read the article. Answer these questions.

1. Give one example of Americans working together to accomplish a difficult task in the past.

2. Why were team sports organizations created in the United States?

3. Besides the players, who are team sports also meant for?

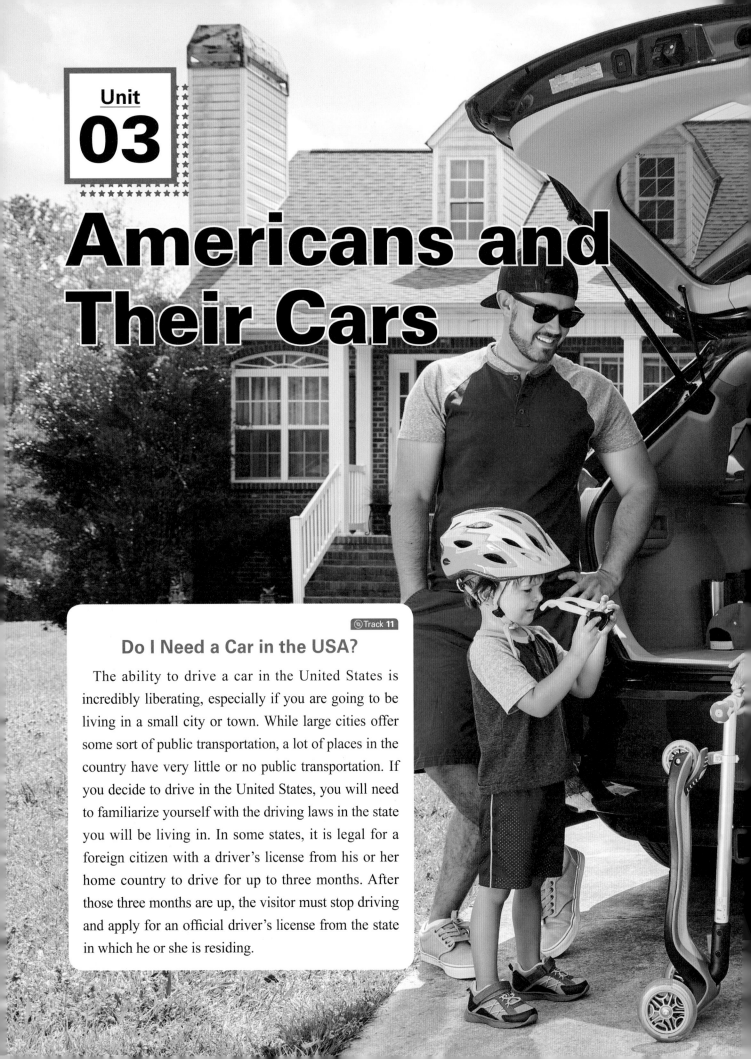

Americans and Their Cars

🔊 Track **11**

Do I Need a Car in the USA?

The ability to drive a car in the United States is incredibly liberating, especially if you are going to be living in a small city or town. While large cities offer some sort of public transportation, a lot of places in the country have very little or no public transportation. If you decide to drive in the United States, you will need to familiarize yourself with the driving laws in the state you will be living in. In some states, it is legal for a foreign citizen with a driver's license from his or her home country to drive for up to three months. After those three months are up, the visitor must stop driving and apply for an official driver's license from the state in which he or she is residing.

Discuss the following questions.

1. Do you know how to drive a car? If yes, when did you get your driver's license?
2. How many times did you take your driver's test before you passed it?
3. How often do you drive?

Other states do not accept foreign driver's licenses at all and require those visiting from other countries to obtain a state driver's license from the state they will be living in. In order to obtain a driver's license, most states require applicants to take a written, or computerized, exam and a driving test at their city's Department of Motor Vehicles (DMV). The computerized exam can be taken at a kiosk at the DMV. Upon completion of the exam, you will be able to check your results immediately. The driving test, also known as the behind-the-wheel test, is usually taken at the city's DMV driving course. An evaluator sits in the passenger's seat and gives you a series of driving tasks which you must perform at a satisfactory level in order to receive a passing grade. By passing your written exam, behind-the-wheel test, and vision test, you will then be able to get your state driver's license.

Conversation ❶ *At the DMV*

A If you plan to drive in the United States, you will need to do some research about the driving laws in the particular state where you plan to live. Each state has different rules and requirements. This is a conversation between a man and a Department of Motor Vehicles worker. Listen and practice the conversation with a partner.

Jaehyun is asking a worker at the DMV for information about obtaining a driver's license.

Worker How can I help you?

Jaehyun I'd like to get a driver's license, but I'm not sure what I need to do.

Worker Are you a U.S. citizen?

Jaehyun No, I'm not. I'm Korean, and I'm in the country on a student visa.

Worker Do you have your passport with you right now?

Jaehyun Yes, I do. Here it is.

Worker Do you have proof of residence?

Jaehyun No, I don't, but I can get it from my landlord.

Worker Okay. Here's the California driver's handbook. Study the information in it and come back with your passport and proof of residence. Then, you can take the written exam.

Jaehyun Can I get my license then?

Worker Once you pass the written exam, you'll be able to make an appointment for your behind-the-wheel test. After you pass the driving test, you'll be able to get your California state driver's license. But be careful.

Jaehyun Careful about what?

Worker If you fail the driving test three times, you have to take the written exam again.

Jaehyun Okay, I see. Thank you very much for your help.

⊘ **Words to Know** citizen visa proof of residence landlord

B Practice the conversation with a partner. Use the information in the box below.

A How can I help you?

B I'd like to get a ¹＿＿＿＿＿ license, but I'm not sure what I need to do.

A Are you a U.S. citizen?

B No, I'm not. I'm ²＿＿＿＿＿, and I'm in the country on a ³＿＿＿＿＿ visa.

1	2	3
commercial driver's	Japanese	work
motorcycle	Korean	domestic employee
marriage	Chinese	tourist

Language Focus

A When visiting the United States as a non-citizen, you must have a visa. Here is a list of the visa types that are available to non-citizens. Look at the chart.

Non-immigrant Visa Types (temporary)		Immigrant Visa Types (permanent)
tourist visa	business visa	immediate relative
student visa	exchange visitor visa	family sponsored
transit/ship crew visa	religious worker visa	spouse of a U.S. citizen
domestic employee visa	journalist and media visa	intercountry adoption

B Read the sentences and write "NIV" if the situation merits a non-immigrant visa type or "IV" if the situation merits an immigrant visa type.

1. Yvonne wants to visit the United States for three weeks.

Her plan is to go to Universal Studios, Six Flags, and Disney Land in California.

2. Minju and Alex were married in Korea and lived there for ten years.

Now, they want to move to Alex's hometown, Minneapolis, Minnesota.

3. Kenji works for a large electronics company in Japan.

His boss is sending him to Chicago, Illinois for five days for a series of meetings.

4. Padma finished her bachelor of arts in India.

Now, she wants to get a master's degree at New York University.

5. Jasmine has just graduated from university in the Philippines.

Now, she has agreed to become a nanny for a wealthy couple's two children in New York City.

6. Ying's brother was born in the United States, but she was not.

Ying would like to become a citizen of the United States, too.

Speak Out | Class Activity

Choose one of the visa types above and do online research about what documentation and other requirements are necessary in order to obtain the visa. Then, tell a classmate about what you discovered during your research.

Visa Type	
Documents	
Other Requirements	

To obtain a tourist visa, you need a passport and an airline ticket.

Conversation ② *Learning to Drive*

Track 13

A If you want to learn to drive, you should find an experienced professional that can teach you the rules of the road. This is a conversation between a driving instructor and a student. Listen and practice the conversation with a partner.

Maria is taking her first driving lesson with a driving instructor.

Instructor	Okay, Maria. What do we need to do first?
Maria	Turn on the engine?
Instructor	Nope. We need to put something on first for safety.
Maria	Oh, we need to put on our seatbelts.
Instructor	Exactly. Now, you can start the engine.
Maria	All right.
Instructor	Now, I want you to put your left turn signal on, put the car in drive, and pull out slowly onto the main road.
Maria	Okay, here we go.
Instructor	You forgot to check your mirror and to look over your shoulder. What if a car were coming? You would have hit that car.
Maria	I'm sorry.
Instructor	That's okay. Pull up to the next intersection and turn right.
Maria	Okay. I'm turning right.
Instructor	Did you remember to put your right blinker on?
Maria	No.
Instructor	How will the other drivers know you are turning right if you don't use your turn signals? Put on your right blinker and pull over to the side of the road.

⊘ **Words to Know** engine seatbelt turn signal intersection

B Practice the conversation with a partner. Use the information in the box below.

A Pull up to the next ¹ _____ and ² _____ .

B Okay. I'm doing it.

A Did you remember to ³ _____ ?

B No. Sorry.

1	2	3
cross street	turn left	stop at the stop sign
stop sign	turn right	look both ways before turning
traffic light	make a left	put your blinker on

Language Focus

A You may encounter a lot of different phrasal verbs when conversing with native English speakers. Phrasal verbs usually consist of a verb and a preposition or a verb and an adverb. Here are a few examples of common phrasal verbs related to driving. Look at the chart.

Phrasal Verbs	Examples
put on	Before you make a turn, be sure to **put** your blinker **on**.
pull out	A car suddenly **pulled out** in front of me without any warning.
pull over	The police signaled to me to **pull over**.
pull up	She **pulled up** her car at the corner.
cut off	He gets very angry when someone **cuts** him **off**.
drop off	Just **drop** me **off** here.
pick up	I'll **pick** you **up** at six.

B Complete the sentences with the correct phrasal verbs from the chart.

1. Could you pick me _____ at the station?

2. Don't pull _____ yet! There's a car coming.

3. Put _____ your blinker and take the next right turn.

4. Here's your change. Please pull _____ to the next window to get your food.

5. There's a police car behind us. I think he wants us to pull _____ .

6. Oh, my gosh! That car just cut me _____ !

7. Can you drop me _____ at school on your way to work?

Speak Out | Group Work

Make a group of four or five students. Then, discuss the questions below. Give reasons for your answers to the questions.

1. Have you ever driven a car in a country outside your own?

2. Do you own a car? If yes, what kind of car is it? If not, what is your dream car?

3. Have you ever been involved in a car accident? If yes, what happened? Were you driving?

4. Do you always put your seatbelt on when you are driving or riding in a car?

5. Have you ever been fined for a traffic violation? If yes, what was the reason?

Conversation ③ *Buying a Used Car*

A There are some important questions you should ask a car salesperson when buying a car in America. It might even be a good idea to bring a friend who knows a lot about cars with you so that you do not end up with a lemon*. Listen and practice the conversation with a partner.

* a lemon: a newly purchased used car with many problems

Wooseong is looking at cars at a used car lot.

Saleswoman So, what are you looking for?

Wooseong Something reliable and affordable.

Saleswoman I have a great mid-sized sedan you might be interested in. Would you like to take a look?

Wooseong Absolutely. Can you tell me the make, model, and year?

Saleswoman It's a 2002 Toyota Corolla. Here it is.

Wooseong What's the mileage?

Saleswoman It has 130,000 miles on it, but it's almost twenty years old.

Wooseong How much are you asking for it?

Saleswoman We're asking $2,700. Is that in your price range?

Wooseong I think it's a bit overpriced.

Saleswoman You do? Well, I happen to know that this car had only one previous owner. I can show you the paperwork if you'd like to see the vehicle history report.

Wooseong Yes, I'd like that. Can I take it for a test drive?

Saleswoman Of course. It purrs like a kitten. The previous owner took really good care of it by getting regular oil changes and regular tune-ups.

Wooseong I'm glad to hear that.

⊘ **Words to Know**   sedan   mileage   overpriced   purr   tune-up

B Practice the conversation with a partner. Use the information in the box below.

A I'm looking for a reliable and ¹ _____ used car.

B I have a great ² _____ you might be interested in. Would you like to take a look?

A Absolutely. Can you tell me the make, model, and year?

B It's a ³ _____ .

1	2	3
safe	minivan	2012 Chrysler Pacifica
sporty	convertible	2014 Mini Cooper
fast	sportscar	2018 Dodge Charger

Language Focus

A We categorize cars by their make, model, and year. A car's value usually decreases the older it gets and the higher the mileage is. Look at the chart for some examples of makes, models, years, and mileages.

Make *Carmaker	Model *Type of car, van, or truck	Year *The year the car was new	Mileage *The number of miles the car has already been driven
• Hyundai • Kia • Toyota • Ford	• Ford F150 • Chrysler Pacifica • Toyota Camry • Volkswagen Passat	• 2013 • 2016 • 2017 • 2020	• 10,000 (very low) • 35,000 (low) • 100,000 (moderate) • 200,000 (high)

B Go online and find four different makes and models of cars for sale on used car sites. Write information about them in the table.

1.

Make _____

Model _____

Year _____

Mileage _____

2.

Make _____

Model _____

Year _____

Mileage _____

3.

Make _____

Model _____

Year _____

Mileage _____

4.

Make _____

Model _____

Year _____

Mileage _____

Speak Out | Pair Work

Imagine you have $15,000 to spend on a car. Find a partner. Then, let your partner tell you about the four used cars, vans, or trucks in his or her table above. Offer to buy one of them. Don't accept your partner's first offer. Negotiate a better price. What kind of car did you buy? Write the make, model, year, mileage, and price that you paid in the table.

Make	Model	Year	Mileage	Price

I have a 2010 Toyota Prius, and it has 5,000 miles on it. You can get it for $ _____ .

I can only spend up to $ _____ . Could I get a bit of a discount?

Wrap It Up

Vocabulary Check Fill in the blanks with the correct answers.

1. Jinny asks everyone in her car to put on their _____ . ⓐ turn signals ⓑ seatbelts

2. Be careful! This is a busy _____ . ⓐ intersection ⓑ engine

3. My car's making strange sounds. I think it needs a _____ . ⓐ mileage ⓑ tune-up

4. My student _____ expires on the 20th of June. ⓐ visa ⓑ proof

5. My _____ wants me to pay the rent on the first of the month.

   ⓐ citizen ⓑ landlord

Situation Talk

A **Role-play the following situation with a partner.**

You are a driving instructor. You are teaching a student how to drive.

1. Ask B what he or she should do first.
2. Tell B that he or she is incorrect. Tell B to put his or her seatbelt on.
3. Tell B that he or she can start the car. Tell B to turn on his or her left turn signal and pull out onto the main road.
4. Tell B to go straight and to turn right at the intersection.
5. Tell B that he or she made a nice turn.

You are in the car with your driving instructor, and you are driving.

1. Say that you think you should start the car.
2. Say okay. Ask A if you can start the car now.
3. Say okay.
4. Say okay. Tell A that you are putting your right turn signal on and making the turn.
5. Say thank you.

B **Look at the four different kinds of cars. Number them from 1 to 4 with 1 being your favorite and 4 being your least favorite. Then, make a group of four students and share your rankings. Tell your group members why you ranked them in that order.**

Sportscar

Minivan

Compact

Sedan

I ranked the sportscar number one because it's my dream to own a sportscar. Red is also my favorite color. I will feel cool if I drive this car.

The Benefits of Carpooling

`Track 15`

Carpooling is when your colleagues and you agree to take turns driving to work in the mornings and back home in the evenings. There are a number of advantages related to carpooling, although it may take a little longer for you to get to work and back home because you have to drive your coworkers.

First, it is good for the environment. Let's say there are four people in your carpool. Instead of four different people in four different cars all going to the same place, there would be four individuals in one car all heading to the same location. The exhaust fumes that would have been emitted from four cars are now only emitted from one car. You have cut down the amount of pollution by seventy-five percent. If you decide to carpool, try to find those who live in and around your neighborhood. If you spend too much time on the road picking each person up, it will defeat the purpose of the carpool.

The second benefit of the carpool is that you will save money on gasoline. All four people in your carpool group would have to pay for their own gasoline if they were driving alone, but if you are sharing rides, you are not paying for gasoline when it is not your turn to drive. Not only is carpooling good for the environment, but it is good for your bank account, too!

The last reason that carpooling is a good practice is that you can become closer with those that you work with. For some people, making friends can be difficult. However, if you put yourself in a situation like a carpool, you will be forced into a social situation where you are very likely to build relationships and become friends with those in your carpool. For these reasons, carpooling is a great way to take care of the planet, to save money, and to make new friends. Hooray for carpooling!

Read the article. Check T for true or F for false.
1. Carpooling is a good way to reduce car emissions and to make city air cleaner. T ☐ / F ☐
2. Carpooling is good for the environment but is more expensive than driving alone. T ☐ / F ☐
3. Carpooling is a good way to build closer relationships with your colleagues. T ☐ / F ☐

Guns in America

Discuss the following questions.

1. How do you feel about hunting and hunters?
2. Have you ever been hunting? Do you think you would like to go hunting?
3. Do you enjoy indoor or outdoor activities? Why?

America's Odd Relationship with Guns

One of the most baffling aspects of American culture for those who did not grow up there is the country's relationship with firearms. Those outside the United States cannot understand why citizens in the USA would tolerate the level of gun violence and mass shootings that continually occur on what seems like an almost daily basis. The answer to this question is complicated, but it involves the American Supreme Court's current interpretation of the 2nd Amendment of the Constitution of the United States, which says that citizens have the right to keep and bear arms.

Additionally, many Americans are outdoor sportsmen and sportswomen. Outdoor sportsmanship includes hunting and fishing. Some Americans hunt by using rifles while others use bows and arrows. Regardless of the weapon one chooses to hunt with, hunting for deer, elk, moose, duck, and pheasant is extremely popular with a lot of Americans. Gun ownership is necessary for some of those who enjoy sport hunting. The downside of this hobby is that just as guns can be used to end the lives of wild animals, they can also be used for more nefarious purposes, such as ending the life of a human being. This issue is a very contentious one in the United States and is sure to be debated for years to come.

Conversation 1 *Talking about Hunting*

A A good number of Americans enjoy outdoor sports like hunting and fishing. Unlike basketball and soccer, hunting is somewhat controversial. Some people see it is as a cruel activity while others insist it is necessary to keep animal populations at a manageable level. In this dialogue, a student and his teacher are discussing a hunting trip. Listen and practice the conversation with a partner.

🔊 Track 17

Jinho is talking to his English professor before class.

Professor Good morning, Jinho. I like your T-shirt. It's nice to meet another hunter.

Jinho Oh, I'm not a hunter. All my T-shirts were dirty, so I borrowed one of my roommate's.

Professor Are you interested in trying hunting sometime?

Jinho I'm not sure. What animals do you hunt here?

Professor It's deer hunting season right now.

Jinho It's illegal to kill deer in my country.

Professor In this state, it's important that some of the deer are killed.

Jinho Why?

Professor If the deer population becomes too high, they starve to death during winter because there isn't enough food for all of them to eat.

Jinho I didn't know that. Unfortunately, I'm not allowed to get a gun license right now.

Professor Why not?

Jinho It's illegal to handle a firearm if you're staying in the U.S. on a student visa.

Professor Oh, I didn't know that. Maybe we can go fishing instead.

Jinho Now that sounds like fun!

> **Words to Know** hunter population starve firearm

T-shirt graphic:
- EAT
- SLEEP
- HUNTING
- REPEAT

B Practice the conversation with a partner. Use the information in the box below.

A I like your T-shirt. It's nice to meet another ¹ _____.

B Oh, I'm not a ¹ _____. All my shirts were dirty, so I borrowed one of my roommate's.

A ² _____ sometime?

B I'm not sure.

A It's ³ _____ season right now.

1	2	3
fisherman	Would you like to try it	bass
bow hunter	What do you think about trying it	elk
hunter	Do you want to try it	duck

Language Focus

A You may meet someone during your time in the States who invites you to try something new or something that he or she thinks you would enjoy. Here are some expressions people use to invite someone to try something new.

Inviting Someone to Try Something New	Common Responses
Would you like to try a French dish this evening?	I'd love to.
Are you interested in trying hunting sometime?	That sounds great.
Have you thought about trying bungee jumping?	That sounds like fun.
What do you think about trying snowboarding?	I'm not sure.
Do you want to try out a new hairstyle?	I don't think I'd like that.

B Complete the questions with expressions from the chart. Then, circle "Yes" or "No" to indicate whether or not you would like to try the activities. Give reasons to support your answers.

1. _____ to try fishing?

Yes / No   Reason: *It's boring to wait quietly for a long time.*

2. _____ to try duck hunting?

Yes / No   Reason: _____

3. _____ in trying sky diving?

Yes / No   Reason: _____

4. _____ about trying bow hunting?

Yes / No   Reason: _____

Speak Out | Group Work

Write four questions about trying something new by using the expressions above. Then, make groups of four or five students. Conduct a survey of your group. The first question has been given as a sample.

Activity	Number of Students
Are you interested in trying hot yoga?	

Which activity was the most popular? Why?

Conversation ② *An Open-carry State*

Track 18

A In the United States, you may find yourself in a situation where someone in your immediate vicinity is carrying a handgun on his or her person. This may be quite shocking for you to experience. Are people allowed to carry guns in public in your country? Listen and practice the conversation with a partner.

Juhee is surprised to see a man carrying a gun in a coffee shop.

Evan	How's your latte?
Juhee	It's great. They make good coffee here.
Evan	It's my favorite café in Austin.
Juhee	Oh, my gosh!
Evan	What's wrong?
Juhee	That man over there has a gun.
Evan	Where?
Juhee	Sitting over there. There's a gun on his belt, but he isn't wearing a uniform. Is he a plainclothes police officer?
Evan	I don't think so. He's probably just a civilian.
Juhee	Why does he have a gun?
Evan	Texas is an open-carry state.
Juhee	What does open-carry mean?
Evan	It means that you can legally carry a gun out in the open if you have a license for it.
Juhee	The man with the gun really makes me nervous. Can we leave?
Evan	If it makes you uncomfortable, we can take our drinks to go.

⊘ **Words to Know**   plainclothes   civilian   open-carry

B Practice the conversation with a partner. Use the information in the box below.

A What does open-carry mean?

B It means that you can ¹ _____ carry a gun out in the open if you have a license for it.

A The man with the gun really makes me ² _____ . Can we ³ _____ ?

B Of course.

1	2	3
lawfully	scared	go
rightfully	uncomfortable	get out of here
legitimately	nervous	take off

Language Focus

A While spending time in the U.S., you might find yourself faced with a situation which makes you uncomfortable. It is absolutely normal to voice your discomfort with the situation to your friends and to take action in order to leave the uncomfortable situation. Here are some common feelings and expressions you can use when faced with these kinds of situations.

Negative Feelings	Desired Actions
It makes me uncomfortable.	Can we leave?
It makes me feel scared.	I'd like to go somewhere else.
It is making me nervous.	Can we take off?
It makes me feel disgusted.	I'd like to get out of here.

B Complete the sentences with negative feelings. Then, write the desired actions.

1. The man with the gun makes me _____ .

2. This area of town is making me _____ .

3. The drunken man makes me feel _____ .

4. The smell makes me feel _____ .

Speak Out

Imagine you are the people in the photos. State your feelings and your desired actions.

The dog makes me really uncomfortable.
Can we take off?

Conversation ③ *First-person Shooter Games*

Track 19

A **Video games are extremely popular in the United States. First-person shooter (FPS) games are among the most popular kinds of games played by gamers in the USA. Are FPS games popular in your country? Listen and practice the conversation with a partner.**

Junyoung and Pichitra are talking about first-person shooter video games.

Pichitra   Hey, Junyoung. Do you like FPS games?

Junyoung   Oh, yeah. I love them.

Pichitra   A group of us play Fortnite in the dormitory in the evenings. Would you like to play with us?

Junyoung   I'd love to, but what about our English homework?

Pichitra   We can do it together before we play.

Junyoung   In that case, sure. Where should we meet?

Pichitra   Which floor do you live on in the dormitory?

Junyoung   I'm on the 1st floor.

Pichitra   I'm on the 1st floor, too.

Junyoung   How's that possible? The 1st floor is the men's floor.

Pichitra   Oh, right. I forgot. What we call the 1st floor in Thailand is actually the 2nd floor in America. Take the lift to the 2nd floor at 5:30. I'm in room 11.

Junyoung   What's a lift?

Pichitra   *(laughing)* The elevator! When we finish studying, we'll play Fortnite. Don't forget your laptop!

Junyoung   Okay. Sounds great!

✅ **Words to Know**   dormitory   lift   laptop

B **Practice the conversation with a partner. Use the information in the box below.**

A   Do you like ¹_____ ?

B   I don't know. What are they?

A   They're ²_____ .

B   Oh, yeah. I love them.

A   A group of my friends play in the ³_____ in the evenings. Would you like to play with us?

1	2	3
RPGs	role-playing games	student union
HOGs	hidden-object games	library
TMGs	time-management games	international student center

Language Focus

A If you visit the United Kingdom and Australia, you will notice some small differences between British English and American English. Below are examples of some common differences.

American English		British English	
5th floor		4th floor	
4th floor		3rd floor	
3rd floor		2nd floor	
2nd floor		1st floor	
ground floor / 1st floor		ground floor	
American	**British**	**American**	**British**
elevator	lift	shopping cart	trolley
apartment	flat	garbage	rubbish
taxi	cab	eraser	rubber
subway	underground	French fries	chips
bar	pub	candy	sweets

B Write the correct words in the blanks.

	American	British		American	British
1.	subway	_____	**2.**	_____	chips
3.	_____	flat	**4.**	eraser	_____
5.	candy	_____	**6.**	garbage	_____
7.	_____	lift	**8.**	taxi	_____
9.	shopping cart	_____	**10.**	_____	pub

Speak Out | Pair Work

Look at the sentences in British English in the right column and rewrite them with the American meanings in the left column. Then, find a partner and compare your answers.

American English	British English
Put the luggage in the trunk of the car.	Put the luggage in the **boot** of the car.
	She drives a **lorry** professionally.
	Would you like a **biscuit**?
	They parked in the **carpark**.
	Where can I find a **petrol station**?

Wrap It Up

Vocabulary Check Complete the sentences by using the words in the box.

plainclothes	firearm	population	dormitory	civilians

1. India has the highest tiger _____ in the world.
2. A _____ police officer chased the man into a subway car.
3. Hundreds of _____ were killed in the battle.
4. The _____ regulations require students to return by 12 o'clock.
5. In Arizona, any citizen over age 21 can carry a _____ in public.

Situation Talk

A **Role-play the following situation with a partner.**

Role A

You are speaking with your classmate, B.

1. Ask B if he or she has ever been hunting.
2. Ask B if he or she would be interested in trying it.
3. Tell B that you didn't know that. Ask B if he or she would like to go fishing instead.

Role B

You are speaking with your classmate, A.

1. Tell A that you haven't been hunting.
2. Tell A that you are staying in the United States on a student visa. Say that it would be illegal for you to use a firearm.
3. Tell A that you would like that.

B **Look at the pictures. Then, state your feelings about them and the desired actions you would like to take.**

C **Use the Internet to search for the differences between American and British English. Find and write some words that didn't appear in this unit. Then, share them with a partner.**

American	British	American	British

Mass Shootings in America

Track 20

Mass shootings that seem to be occurring more frequently as of late are one of the most troubling aspects of American culture. The most infamous example is probably the Columbine shooting, which took place in Colorado in 1999 and claimed the lives of thirteen students and teachers at the high school. The more recent Las Vegas mass shooting claimed the lives of an astounding 58 people. In between these two shootings were dozens of other mass shootings. There was one in Newtown, Connecticut, which claimed the lives of 28 elementary school students and teachers, and another racially motivated shooting which took place in Charleston, South Carolina, which claimed the lives of nine African-American church parishioners.

What is so perplexing about these killings to those who live outside the United States is why the country allows them to keep occurring. They wonder why private citizens are allowed to own and carry firearms with enough power to slaughter dozens of innocent people in mere seconds. This is where the issue becomes politicized in the United States and has much to do with the Supreme Court's interpretation of the 2nd Amendment of the Constitution. The 2nd Amendment reads like this: "A well-regulated Militia, being necessary to the security of a free State, the right of the people to keep and bear Arms, shall not be infringed." This one sentence in the Constitution of the United States politically divides the country in half. One side wants to protect the right of private citizens to own guns, and the other side would like to see strict regulation.

Consider these shocking statistics regarding guns in America. The first is that there are approximately 39,000 gun deaths each year. Mass shootings, however, only account for two percent of those deaths. Suicide by gun is by far the most common form of gun death. The second is that there are more than 390 million guns in the United States right now. That is enough for every man, woman, and child to have one, and there would still be tens of millions left over. It should be quite obvious to you by now that America has a serious problem when it comes to gun violence. Americans need to ask themselves how long they intend to tolerate this madness. The rest of the world is watching in astonishment and wondering why the country seems to do absolutely nothing about it.

Read the article. Answer these questions.

1. What does the writer consider to be one of the most troubling aspects of American culture?

2. Why does the U.S. government not take away all of the guns from private citizens?

3. Approximately how many gun deaths are there in the United States each year?

Unit 05

Dating

◎Track 21

Dating in the Digital Age

Just as smartphones have changed dramatically over the past ten years, so has dating. Whereas you once had to meet other single people in more traditional ways, you can now simply swipe right on your smartphone screen to meet someone. Not only will he or she be your physical type, but the person will also be in your immediate vicinity at the time you want to meet. Dating apps like Tinder and OK Cupid make dating in the digital age simple.

Discuss the following questions.

1. Do you have a girlfriend or boyfriend? If so, how did you meet her or him?
2. How do couples usually meet in your country?
3. Are dating apps popular in your country? If so, which ones do single people use to meet other singles?

These platforms allow users to sign up and create profiles within the apps. Then, other users of the apps can log in and view your profile. If they like your picture and comment, they will send you a message and ask you to meet. These apps use your smartphone's global positioning system to determine where the two of you are in relation to one another. If you are in the same vicinity, the app will inform you, and the two of you can decide where to meet.

All of this seems complicated to those from older generations, but dating apps actually make the act of meeting someone much simpler. In fact, it erases the worst part of dating, which is the rejection. You will never know the feeling of walking up to someone, asking the person for his or her phone number, and hearing those awful words, "No, thanks."

Conversation 1 *Are You Flirting with Me?*

Track 22

A As a single person in the United States, you never know when you might meet someone of the opposite sex. Innocent flirting often takes place in situations where one person gives a social cue to the other by way of a glance or a greeting. This is a conversation between a single man and a single woman at a supermarket. Listen and practice the conversation with a partner.

Javier and Leah meet for the first time at the supermarket.

Javier   Hello.

Leah   Hi. I like your accent. Where are you from?

Javier   Are you flirting with me?

Leah   Maybe.

Javier   I'm from Peru, but I've lived in the States for several years now.

Leah   Do you live in this neighborhood?

Javier   Actually, I just moved here about a month ago. It's closer to work.

Leah   What do you do?

Javier   I'm a programmer. And you?

Leah   I'm a fashion designer.

Javier   That makes sense. You're very stylish.

Leah   Thanks.

Javier   Maybe you can help me with something.

Leah   What's that?

Javier   I never know which apples to buy. I either buy them too ripe or not ripe enough.

Leah   They should be firm, but not too firm. Let me help you choose some.

⊘ **Words to Know**   flirt   make sense   ripe   firm

B Practice the conversation with a partner. Use the information in the box below.

A ¹ ....

B Hello. I like your ² .... Where are you from?

A Are you flirting with me?

B Maybe.

A I'm from ³ .... , but I've lived in the States for several years now.

1	2	3
Hey.	shirt	Mexico
How's it going?	glasses	Italy
Hello.	hair	Korea

Language Focus

A Flirting between two people often begins with a glance, a greeting, or even a compliment. You should be careful not to offend the other person and make sure the situation is appropriate. Here are some expressions you can use when complimenting someone. Look at the chart.

Giving Compliments	
I like your hair.	Your dress looks really nice.
I love your shirt.	You look handsome.
I think your shoes are really cool.	You're very beautiful.
I adore your jacket.	You have lovely eyes.
It looks good on you.	That is a stylish watch.

B Give three compliments to each person. Write your compliments in the blanks.

1.

   ① _____

   ② _____

   ③ _____

2.

   ① _____

   ② _____

   ③ _____

Speak Out | Pair Work

Find a partner. Greet your partner casually. Then, compliment him or her. You can use examples from the chart above.

A *Hi.*
B *Hey.*
A *I like your jacket. It looks really nice on you.*
B *Thank you. I adore your shoes. They're very charming.*
A *Thanks.*

Conversation ❷ *Asking Someone Out on a Date*

Track 23

A In American culture, it is still more common for men to ask women out on dates, although it is not uncommon for women to ask men out, too. This is a conversation between a male and a female student. Listen and practice the conversation with a partner.

Eric is asking Hannah, his classmate, out on a date.

Eric	Hannah, hold up a sec.
Hannah	What's up, Eric?
Eric	Are you busy this Saturday?
Hannah	Unfortunately, I'm going to a concert with my roommate.
Eric	Oh, that's cool. How about Friday night?
Hannah	I don't have any plans yet.
Eric	Great. I was wondering if you'd like to get some pizza and then see a movie. I know where the best pizzeria in New York is.
Hannah	Mario's is the best.
Eric	Mario's is good, but the place I know is far superior to Mario's.
Hannah	What time do you want to meet up?
Eric	I thought we could meet in front of the dormitory at 7:00 p.m. That way, we could walk to the pizza place together.
Hannah	Sure, Eric. I'd love to.
Eric	Great. I'll see you then.

⊘ Words to Know   sec (= second)   pizzeria   superior

B Practice the conversation with a partner. Use the information in the box below.

A ¹ .... this Saturday?

B I don't have any plans yet.

A Great. I was wondering if you'd like to get some pizza and then ² .... I know where the best pizzeria in New York is.

B Mario's is the best.

A Mario's is good, but the place I know is ³ .... Mario's.

1	2	3
Are you doing anything	see a play	a million times better than
Do you have any plans for	go to a dance club	far superior to
Are you busy	see a concert	a lot better than

Language Focus

A There are some common expressions that we can use when asking someone out on a date or when being asked out on a date. Look at the expressions in the chart.

Asking Someone Out on a Date	Accepting or Rejecting a Date Request
Do you have any plans on Saturday? Are you busy on Friday? Are you doing anything on Wednesday? I was wondering if you'd like to go out with me.	I'm free on Saturday. Unfortunately, I have plans on Friday. I'm sorry, but I'm busy on Wednesday. Actually, I have a boyfriend/girlfriend.
Suggesting a Time and Place	**Accepting or Rejecting a Suggestion**
How about meeting at the mall at 8 o'clock? Let's meet at noon at the coffee shop. Does 7:30 work for you?	The mall at 8 o'clock sounds great! Okay. See you then. I'm sorry, but I can't meet at 7:30. Can we meet an hour later at 8:30?

B Complete the conversations with the correct words or phrases from the chart. Then, practice them with a partner.

Conversation 1

A Are you ¹ _____ on Saturday, Ann?

B ² _____ , I have plans on Saturday.

A How about Friday?

B I'm ³ _____ on Friday.

A Great. How about ⁴ _____ at the coffee shop at 7 o'clock?

B Sounds good.

Conversation 2

A Are you ⁵ _____ anything on Saturday?

B No, I'm free on Saturday.

A Great. Let's ⁶ _____ at noon in front of the dormitory. I know where a good galbi restaurant is. We can walk there together.

B Okay. See you ⁷ _____ .

Speak Out

Imagine you are the people below, and you are being asked out by someone. Respond appropriately by looking at the facial expressions of the people. Use various expressions from the chart above.

A *Are you busy on Friday, Andi?*

B *No, I'm not. I'm free on Friday.*

Conversation ③ *Using Dating Apps*

ⓑ Track 24

A When using a dating app, we can see a picture of the person we are meeting and send messages to him or her. However, we may not be able to pick him or her out of a crowd because we sometimes look different in pictures than we do in real life. In this dialogue, a man is trying to find a woman he met on a dating app. Listen and practice the conversation with a partner.

Tyler is looking for Maggie, a woman he has just met on a dating app, in a bar.

Tyler	Excuse me. Are you Maggie?
Woman	No, sorry.
Tyler	Would you happen to know anyone named Maggie in the bar?
Woman	No, I don't know anyone named Maggie.
Tyler	Sorry to bother you.

Tyler continues looking around the bar for Maggie when he hears his name.

Maggie	Are you Tyler?
Tyler	Yes, I am.
Maggie	Nice to meet you!
Tyler	Nice to meet you, too!
Maggie	You're cuter than your picture.
Tyler	Thank you. You don't look anything like your picture. You have pink hair.
Maggie	I know. My roommate dyed it earlier this evening. Do you want to do some tequila shots?
Tyler	I'm not a very good drinker.
Maggie	Come on! Don't be a wimp.

⊘ **Words to Know** bother dye tequila wimp

B Practice the conversation with a partner. Use the information in the box below.

A Excuse me. ¹ _____ Maggie?

B No, sorry.

A ² _____ anyone here named Maggie?

B ³ _____ I don't know anyone here named Maggie.

1	2	3
Is your name	Is there	Sorry, but
Do you happen to be	Do you know if there is	I have no idea.
Would you happen to be	Do you happen to know if there is	Sorry, dude, but

Language Focus

A There are some common expressions that you can use when trying to find someone you have never met in person. Sometimes, you may have to ask a stranger if that person knows the whereabouts of the person you are looking for. Look at the expressions in the chart.

Asking Someone If He or She Is the Person You Are Looking for	Are you Brian? Is your name Melissa? Do you happen to be Kenzo? Would you happen to be Hyunsu?
Asking the Whereabouts of Someone You Are Looking for	Is there anyone here named Katrina? Do you know if there is anyone named Bob here? Would you happen to know if John is here?
Saying Whether You Know the Whereabouts of Someone	Sorry, but I don't know anyone named Katrina. I have no idea. I don't know anyone named Bob. Sorry, dude, but I just got here.

B Complete the dialogues by using the expressions from the chart.

Sorry, but I don't know anyone named Maggie.

1. _____ named Maggie?

2. _____ Tyler?

Yes, I am. Nice to meet you!

Speak Out | Pair Work

Find a partner. Imagine you are looking for a person below at a bar. Try to find the person by asking your partner. Switch roles and repeat the exercise. Use various expressions above.

 Byron
 Sarah
 Wong
Sujin

A *Are you Byron?*
B *No, sorry.*
A *Would you happen to know if Byron is here?*
B *I have no idea. I don't know anyone named Byron.*

Wrap It Up

Match the words with their correct definitions.

1. bother •
2. ripe •
3. superior •
4. flirt •
5. wimp •

• ⓐ better than other things of the same kind in quality
• ⓑ someone who is not strong or confident
• ⓒ to annoy someone by interrupting that person
• ⓓ to show romantic affection toward or interest in another person
• ⓔ the point where fruit or vegetables are ready to be eaten

Situation Talk

A **Role-play the following situation with a partner.**

You are asking B out on a date.

1. Ask B if you can talk to him or her for a sec.
2. Ask B if he or she is busy on Friday night.
3. Ask B if he or she has any plans on Saturday night.
4. Ask B if he or she would like to get dinner and then see a play.
5. Ask B if 6 p.m. works for him or her.
6. Ask B if he or she likes Korean food.

A is asking you out on a date.

1. Tell A that you can talk. Ask A what is up.
2. Tell A that you have plans on Friday night.
3. Tell A that you don't have any plans yet.
4. Say okay. Ask A what time he or she would like to go out.
5. Tell A that 6 p.m. works for you. Ask A what kind of restaurant he or she wants to go to.
6. Tell A that you love Korean food.

B **Take one of the names in the chart below for yourself. Make sure everyone has a different name, and don't forget your name. Finally, have your teacher choose two names, one man and one woman. All of the students should stand up and mingle as if the classroom were a bar. If the teacher says your name, you must find the other person in the classroom by asking the names of the other students in the class.**

Anna	Heather	Alex	Frank
Becky	Jackie	Brian	John
Cara	Kristie	Chris	Michael
Diane	Lisa	Daniel	Ryan
Fiona	Sarah	Eric	Zach

Dating: Who Pays?

🔊 Track 25

Dating in America can present a multitude of obstacles, especially for those who are not familiar with the culture. One of the first questions you might ask yourself is who should pay for this date? Should I pay because I am the man, or should she pay because she asked me out? Should we go Dutch? If so, how do I ask her for half the bill without looking like a jerk? These issues become even more important if you are strapped for cash but want to go out with that guy or girl in your class that you really like.

There are dating gurus in the media who will give you the "5 Rules for Dating" or "3 Things Never to Do on a Date." Ignore these people and relax. Remember that you are just two human beings who want to spend time with one another. If, in fact, the person you are going out with is only interested in your money, then you probably want to find another partner anyway. Although there are not any hard and fast rules that you have to live by, there are some simple guidelines you can follow in order to reduce anxiety.

If a man asks a woman out, then the man is expected to pay for the date in American culture. In this case, the man should choose a restaurant or activity that he can afford and will not break the bank. This could include a picnic in the park or a hike. These are activities that can be fun and do not require lots of money. If a woman asks a man out on a date, then she should be expected to pay, although some men will insist on paying anyway. If the man insists, let him pay. If the man is a student and does not have a lot of money, the woman will often offer to pay or to split the bill with him. She might even suggest activities that do not cost much money. The point is that if two people really like each other, they will figure out a way to be together even if there is not a lot of money between the two of them. Love always finds a way!

Read the article. Check T for true or F for false.

1. In American culture, the man should always pay for the first date. T ☐ / F ☐
2. Following the advice of dating gurus in the media is the best way to have a successful date. T ☐ / F ☐
3. If the man does not have a lot of money, the woman will often offer to split the bill. T ☐ / F ☐

Unit
06

Travel in America

Track 26

Traveling Domestically

Domestic travel is very popular in the United States. The country is vast enough that residents can visit states such as Alaska and Hawaii and feel as if they have just been to foreign countries. Even within the lower 48 states, there are several different regions with different weather patterns and subcultures which people find interesting.

In the mainland United States, the east and west coasts are the most popular tourist spots. On the west coast, Los Angeles, California has a robust tourism industry with its multiple movie studios and theme parks. The climate in Los Angeles is usually quite amenable for travel. The temperature is relatively comfortable all year round, and even when it is hot, it is a dry heat. Unlike the southeast region of the United States, California has low humidity, even in the summer.

Discuss the following questions.

1. Do you prefer traveling abroad or traveling within your own country? Why?
2. Have you ever traveled abroad? If so, which countries did you visit?
3. How often do you travel? Do you usually travel for fun, for work, or both? Explain your answer.

On the east coast, New York City is, of course, a very popular travel destination due to its cultural importance in the world. You can visit the Statue of Liberty, the Empire State Building, Central Park, and Times Square, all locations familiar with a majority of the world's population.

Overall, it is not uncommon for many Americans to live their entire lives without ever having a passport. These travelers find traveling within the United States comfortable and satisfying. Never having to deal with language and cultural barriers is a big incentive for them to travel within the United States.

Conversation ① *A Day Trip*

A Day trips are very popular for Americans. A day trip occurs when you visit a travel location that is not too far from your home and you return home the same day instead of staying overnight at a hotel. This is a conversation between a couple who is planning a day trip. Listen and practice the conversation with a partner.

Simon and Jina are planning a day trip to Joshua Tree in California.

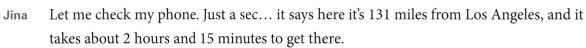

Simon What should we do this coming Saturday, Jina?

Jina We didn't do anything this past Saturday, so I think a day trip to Joshua Tree would be really cool.

Simon Last Saturday, we went to a movie.

Jina I know, but I want to do something outside this weekend.

Simon Okay. How far is Joshua Tree from Los Angeles? We can take my car.

Jina Let me check my phone. Just a sec… it says here it's 131 miles from Los Angeles, and it takes about 2 hours and 15 minutes to get there.

Simon Should we stop and eat on the way or pack a lunch?

Jina Why don't we pack a lunch? We can leave early at around six o'clock. Then, we can visit some of the palm oases, hike up to the top of a nice peak, and have lunch there.

Simon That sounds lovely. Let's remember to bring lots of water. It gets hot in the desert.

Jina Don't worry. I'll bring lots of water.

Simon Great. I'll have my car, so if we get too tired, we can just head home.

⊘ **Words to Know** pack palm peak desert

B Practice the conversation with a partner. Use the information in the box below.

A What should we do ¹_____?

B I don't know. I think a day trip to ²_____ would be really cool.

A How long does it take from Los Angeles by car?

B It takes about ³_____ to get there.

1	2	3
next Saturday	Palm Springs	an hour and forty minutes
this Saturday	Santa Barbara	50 minutes
two weeks from this Saturday	San Diego	two hours

Language Focus

The language regarding a particular day in a schedule can be confusing to non-native English speakers. Look at some time expressions you can use to make plans. Then, match the expressions with the correct days in the calendar.

ⓐ next Saturday / a week from this Saturday
ⓒ two weeks from this Saturday
ⓔ this Saturday / this coming Saturday
ⓖ last Monday / the Monday before this past Monday

ⓑ this past Sunday
ⓓ tomorrow
ⓕ yesterday

Sun	Mon	Tue	Wed	Thu	Fri	Sat
30	31 (¹ ⓖ)	1	2	3	4	5
6 (²)	7	8 (³)	9 today	10 (⁴)	11	12 (⁵)
13	14	15	16	17	18	19 (⁶)
20	21	22	23	24	25	26 (⁷)

Speak Out | Pair Work

Find a partner. Then, take turns asking each other what Bora is doing on the dates below by using the expressions above.

Bora's Calendar

S	M	T	W	T	F	S
			1	2	3	
4 a general house cleaning	5 bowling	6	7	8	9	10 Six Flags
11	12 meeting	13 today	14 work dinner	15	16	17 Joshua Tree
18 shopping	19	20	21	22	23 Juhee's birthday party	24 Universal Studios
25	26	27	28 the movies	29 PARTY	30	31

A *What is Bora doing two weeks from this Thursday?*
B *She is going to a party.*

Conversation ② *A Weekend Getaway*

Track 28

A Traveling within the country is very popular with Americans because the country is quite large and interesting places to visit exist all across the country. This is a conversation between a couple who is planning a weekend getaway. Listen and practice the conversation with a partner.

Joe is telling Melanie about a weekend getaway he has planned for the two of them.

Joe	Clear your calendar for this weekend.
Melanie	Why?
Joe	I made plans for us.
Melanie	What are they?
Joe	I made a reservation at a bed and breakfast in New Hampshire. It's supposed to be really beautiful there in the fall.
Melanie	Oh, no! It's my roommate's birthday this weekend. We're supposed to go clubbing.
Joe	It's okay. I spoke with her and explained that this Saturday is the one-year anniversary of our first date. But I promised we'd take her out next weekend.
Melanie	Are you sure she's okay with it?
Joe	You know Bonnie. She's very laid back.
Melanie	You've thought of everything.
Joe	Not everything. Do you think your dad would let us use his car for the weekend? Mine's in the shop.
Melanie	I'm sure he'd be okay with it.

✅ **Words to Know** getaway   go clubbing   anniversary   laid back

B Practice the conversation with a partner. Use the information in the box below.

A Clear your calendar for ¹ _____ .

B Why?

A I made plans for us.

B What are they?

A I ² _____ at ³ _____ .

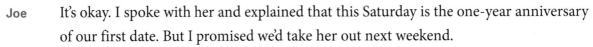

1	2	3
the week of the 15th	booked us a suite	a fancy hotel in Miami
the weekend of the 24th	reserved a campsite	a popular national park
next weekend	reserved a bungalow	an exotic resort in Thailand

Language Focus

A There are several kinds of trips that are common in the USA. There are also different kinds of accommodations you can choose. Look at the chart.

Types of Trips, Holidays, and Vacations	Types of Accommodations
day trip	hotel
weekend getaway	motel
family vacation	inn
hometown visit	bed and breakfast (B&B)
romantic holiday / honeymoon	lodge
camping trip / backpacking trip	youth hostel

B Match the words with the correct pictures.

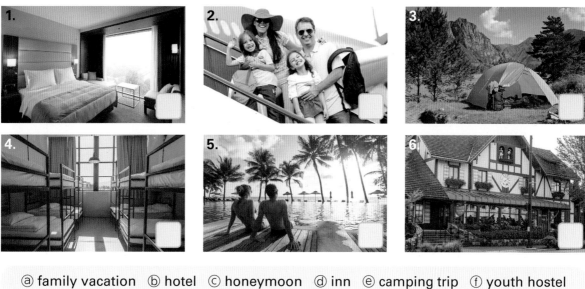

ⓐ family vacation ⓑ hotel ⓒ honeymoon ⓓ inn ⓔ camping trip ⓕ youth hostel

Speak Out | Pair Work

Find a partner. Then, plan a weekend trip by filling in the chart with your trip itinerary. After that, share your trip details with the class.

Our Trip to _____	
Saturday	**Sunday**
Morning:	Morning:
Afternoon:	Afternoon:
Evening:	Evening:
Accommodation Type:	

We planned a trip to New York for this weekend. On Saturday morning, we ...

Conversation ③ *Spring Break*

A Most universities have a weeklong spring break in late March, and lots of students take this opportunity to travel south in the United States in order to enjoy warm weather and beautiful beaches. Some students even take trips to Cancun and Acapulco, Mexico and enjoy the warm weather and the nice beaches there, too. Do universities in your country have a similar situation? Listen and practice the conversation with a partner.

Yuna and Sadie are talking about their upcoming trip to Cancun, Mexico for spring break.

Yuna Sadie, did you remember to get your passport?

Sadie Oh, no! I forgot.

Yuna Spring break is coming up soon, and the tickets are nonrefundable.

Sadie What should I do?

Yuna Let's go to the passport agency and get you a passport ASAP. I can't believe you don't have one.

Sadie I've never needed one because I've never left the United States.

Yuna Really? What about a family vacation or a class trip?

Sadie My parents took us to Niagara Falls one summer, but you don't need a passport to cross the Canadian border.

Yuna Look at this website. It says that for an extra $90, they can expedite the passport process, and you can get it two weeks earlier.

Sadie That's great.

⊘ **Words to Know**   nonrefundable   ASAP   border   expedite

B Practice the conversation with a partner. Use the information in the box below.

A Did you remember to ¹ .... ?

B Oh, no! I forgot.

A ² .... is coming up soon, and the ³ .... are nonrefundable. You'd better do it ASAP!

B Okay. I will.

1	2	3
reserve an Air BNB	Our trip to Daytona Beach	airline tickets
book a hotel	Our vacation	train tickets
ask Angela to watch our cat while we're gone	Spring break	hotel reservations

Language Focus

A Americans use acronyms such ASAP or FYI in everyday speech. An acronym is a grouping of letters in which each letter represents the first letter of each word in the expression. For example, ASAP stands for as soon as possible. Look at the chart.

Common English Acronyms			
ASAP	as soon as possible	**ETA**	estimated time of arrival
AKA	also known as	**FYI**	for your information
ATM	automated teller machine	**RIP**	Rest in peace
AWOL	absent without leave (military acronym)	**RSVP**	Répondez s'il vous plaît. (French)
BRB	be right back	**TBA**	to be announced
DIY	do it yourself	**TGIF**	Thank God It's Friday.

B Complete the sentences with the correct acronyms from the chart.

1. It's a quarter to ten right now. What's our _____?

2. Robert Sherman, _____, Bobby Sherman is a good friend of mine.

3. _____, we're meeting a half an hour later than usual because of the snowstorm.

4. The date and the time of the exam are _____. We should find out sometime next week.

5. Is there an _____ around here? I need to get some cash.

6. My father does a lot of _____ projects around the house, but my mother wishes he would just hire someone to do them properly.

7. Sherry's having a party next Friday. She'd like people to _____ by next Monday.

8. _____! This has been one of the toughest workweeks I've had in a long time.

Speak Out | Class Activity

Read the five questions in the table. Then, ask five different students questions from the table. Make sure to ask each student a different question. Write their answers in the blanks.

Questions	Answers
What is something you need to do ASAP?	
When was the last time you RSVPed to a party?	
Who are you or someone you know AKA?	
When did you last use an ATM?	
Have you ever done a DIY project?	

Wrap It Up

Vocabulary Check Fill in the blanks with the correct answers.

1. Let's climb to the top of the _____.
       ⓐ peak   ⓑ desert

2. Can you _____ the passport process?
       ⓐ nonrefundable   ⓑ expedite

3. The couple is celebrating their two-year _____.
       ⓐ anniversary   ⓑ getaway

4. Call me back _____!
       ⓐ FYI   ⓑ ASAP

5. Paul is always relaxed. He's so _____.
       ⓐ pack   ⓑ laid back

Situation Talk

A   **Role-play the following situation with a partner.**

Role **A**	Role **B**
You are asking your friend what he or she wants to do this weekend.	*You are suggesting a day trip in your state.*
1. Ask B what he or she wants to do this Saturday.	1. Suggest a day trip to Santa Barbara, California.
2. Tell B that you went there the weekend before last.	2. Suggest a trip to Joshua Tree National Park.
3. Tell B that you think it is a great idea. Ask B what time the two of you should leave.	3. Tell A that you two should leave early at around six o'clock. Ask A if the two of you should eat at a restaurant on the way or pack a lunch.
4. Tell B that the two of you should pack a lunch. Suggest hiking to one of the peaks and eating lunch there.	4. Tell A that you think it is a great idea. Offer to drive to Joshua Tree.
5. Thank B for offering to drive. Promise to bring lots of water because it gets very hot there.	5. Tell A that you are excited about the day trip.

B   **Plan your perfect vacation by completing the chart with details. Then, find a partner and share your dream vacation plans with him or her.**

My Dream Vacation

Where to?	Who with?	Where to stay?	Activities?	Total budget?

How about a Staycation?

Track 30

Have you ever returned from a vacation and felt like you needed a vacation from your vacation? If you have ever felt that way and were looking for an alternative to the stresses associated with purchasing airline tickets, booking hotels, and going sightseeing, you might elect to take what some Americans call a staycation. A staycation occurs when you take vacation days off from work but decide to go nowhere. Instead, you take a look around at some of the interesting things you may have missed in your city or neighborhood while you were busy with work and family life.

A lot of Americans are so work-oriented that they never have a chance to visit any of the interesting places that exist right outside their front door. When they have a week or two of vacation, they feel the need to get as far away from home as possible for it to feel like a genuine vacation. These days, a lot of Americans are taking a step back and wondering to themselves why distance seems to override quality in terms of time spent on vacation. If you can relax and enjoy yourself from the comfort of your own home, neighborhood, or city, why not take advantage of that?

There are lots of ways to do a staycation. If you want to have the feeling of getting away but do not want to deal with the hassles related to flying, you can book a nice hotel in your city and spend a few nights there enjoying the hotel's amenities, such as the pool, the hot tub, and the sauna. You will surely be able to find some nice restaurants in your city or even better, opt for room service at the hotel. Regardless of how you decide to spend your staycation, eliminating the aggravations of booking hotels and waiting in line at the airport will truly allow you to unwind and recharge your batteries. And isn't that what a vacation is all about?

Read the article. Answer these questions.

1. What is a staycation?
2. Why do so many Americans not have the chance to see interesting places in their city?
3. According to the article, what is the real purpose of a vacation?

Unit 07

Health Care

⊙ Track 31

Health Insurance in the USA

In America, most health insurance is provided to people through their workplaces. The health insurance that the company provides is considered one of the benefits of working at a company. It is often part of the calculation workers make when accepting or rejecting job offers. It is not uncommon for a worker to accept a lower-paying job because the healthcare plan at one company is better than that at another job which pays a higher wage but provides a weaker healthcare plan.

Health insurance has been tied to employment for many decades in the U.S., and this system is fairly unique when compared to other developed countries. The way the system works is that a company chooses an insurance plan through a health maintenance organization, or an HMO. An HMO is a group of hospitals and doctors in a network that provide care to people in the network when they get sick. Those receiving healthcare from a specific HMO are required to see a doctor within the network of providers covered by that specific HMO.

One of the problems with this system is emergency care. If a person in a serious car accident needs to go to the nearest hospital, one which is not within the person's healthcare network, exorbitant costs can accrue, and those costs are not covered by the person's insurance plan. The costs for a serious injury could reach hundreds of thousands if not millions of dollars.

Discuss the following questions.

1. Does your country have a nationalized health insurance system?
2. How much does it cost to go to the doctor for a cold or the flu?
3. Do you think health insurance should be provided through a person's job? Why or why not?

Conversation 1 *Healthcare Providers*

Track 32

A **Americans are less likely to go to the doctor for minor illnesses compared to people in other countries. One of the reasons for this relates to the costs of copayments in some insurance plans and the high costs of prescription medications in the USA. This is a conversation between a man and his friend who is not feeling well. Listen and practice the conversation with a partner.**

Haeyeon is thinking about going to the doctor's office, but she is consulting her friend Alex first.

Alex	*(phone ringing)* Hello.
Haeyeon	Hey, Alex.
Alex	Your voice sounds hoarse. Are you sick?
Haeyeon	Yeah. I think I've got the flu. What should I do?
Alex	Oh, no. You should go to the doctor.
Haeyeon	Could you give me a ride? I don't have the energy to take the bus.
Alex	I'd be happy to give you a ride to the doctor's office. Who's your primary caregiver?
Haeyeon	I don't know. This is the first time I've gone to the clinic in the U.S.
Alex	Who is your healthcare provider?
Haeyeon	I have an insurance card in my wallet that says Life Partners.
Alex	I have Life Partners, too. I know a nearby clinic that accepts our insurance. The GP there is really good, but you'll have to wait a while because you don't have an appointment.
Haeyeon	That's okay. What's a GP by the way?
Alex	A general practitioner. It means she can diagnose and treat common illnesses. I'll pick you up in ten minutes.
Haeyeon	Thank you so much, Alex. You're a lifesaver.

✅ **Words to Know** hoarse insurance diagnose treat

B **Practice the conversation with a partner. Use the information in the box below.**

A Hey, Alex.

B You sound terrible. Are you ¹ _____ ?

A Yeah. I think I ² _____ .

B Oh, no. ³ _____

1	2	3
hurt	sprained my ankle	You should go to the ER.
sick	have a sore throat	Why don't you go to the doctor?
injured	broke my toe on the coffee table	If I were you, I would go to the hospital.

Language Focus

A   There are times when you become sick or injured, and you are not sure what to do. This is especially true when you are staying in a foreign country and are unfamiliar with the healthcare system in that country. Look at the expressions for giving advice.

Giving Advice	
A I have a headache. What should I do? **B** **You should** take some aspirin.	**A** I fell down, and I think I've broken my wrist. **B** **You'd better** go to the hospital.
A My back hurts. What should I do? **B** **Why don't you** do some stretching?	**A** I'm having chest pains. **B** **If I were you, I would** go to the ER immediately!

B   Give your best advice by using the expressions in the chart. Then, share the answers with a partner.

1. A I've got a really bad headache. What should I do?

   B ....

2. A I lifted some heavy boxes. Now my back hurts. What should I do?

   B ....

3. A I have a really bad sunburn. What should I do?

   B ....

4. A I stubbed my toe on the coffee table. I think it's broken. What should I do?

   B ....

Speak Out | Pair Work

Find a partner. Then, tell your partner you are suffering from one of the ailments below, and let your partner give you advice by using the expressions above. Switch roles and repeat the exercise.

Common Ailments		
I have the flu.	I have a bad sunburn.	I have a headache.
I pulled a muscle.	I have a stomachache.	I have a sore throat.
I cut my finger.	I have indigestion.	I have a cold.
I broke my toe.	I sprained my ankle.	I bruised my shin.

A *I have the flu. What should I do?*
B *I think you should go to the doctor.*

Conversation ❷ *Making a Doctor's Appointment*

A **If you get sick in America, the most efficient way to be seen by a physician is to make an appointment. Most Americans do not go to the hospital for common illnesses. Instead, they go to a clinic where they can be seen by a GP. If the situation is serious, the GP will refer the person to a specialist, a person whose expertise and training center around one specific area of medicine. Listen and practice the conversation with a partner.**

Ben is calling his local clinic in order to make an appointment.

Receptionist	Family Health Clinic. This is Karen. How may I help you?
Ben	*(coughing)* Hi. My name is Ben Larson, and I'd like to make an appointment.
Receptionist	What seems to be the problem?
Ben	I think I've got a sinus infection.
Receptionist	Okay. Who is your insurance provider?
Ben	It's Essential Care.
Receptionist	Great. Dr. Chen has an opening tomorrow at 3:30 p.m.
Ben	Tomorrow at 3:30 p.m.? Isn't there anything sooner than that?
Receptionist	I'm sorry, but that's the soonest he can see you. Could you hold for a moment? I'm getting another call.
Ben	Sure.
Receptionist	*(moments later)* You're in luck. We've just had a cancellation. There's an opening this morning at 10:30 a.m.
Ben	I'll take it!
Receptionist	Okay. Let me get a little more information from you.

⊘ **Words to Know** infection opening cancellation

B **Practice the conversation with a partner. Use the information in the box below.**

A Hi. My name is Ben Larson, and I'd like to make an appointment.

B Okay. Dr. Chen has an opening ¹ ....

A ² .... Isn't there anything sooner than that?

B ³ .... , but that's the soonest he can see you.

1	2	3
this Thursday at 1 p.m.	This Thursday?	I apologize
a week from this Tuesday	That's over a week!	I understand your frustration
today at five o'clock	That late?	Sorry

Language Focus

A   In America, it is very important to make a doctor's appointment if you can. Arriving at the clinic without an appointment might result in a very long wait. Here are some expressions you can use when making an appointment.

Availability	We have an opening on March 2 at two o'clock.
	Are you available this Friday at 9:30 a.m.?
	Is November 11 at one-thirty okay?
	How about tomorrow at three o'clock?
Responding	March 2 at two o'clock is fine.
	Friday at nine-thirty would be perfect.
	The 11th at one-thirty works for me.
	I'm afraid tomorrow is no good.
Cancelling / Rescheduling	I'm afraid I have to cancel my appointment.
	Unfortunately, I am unable to make my appointment. Can I reschedule it?
	Would it be possible for me to change my appointment?

B   Fill in the blanks by using the expressions in the chart for making a doctor's appointment. Then, practice the conversations with a partner.

1. **A** _____ Friday at nine o'clock _____ ?

  B Yes. Nine o'clock on Friday would _____ .

2. **A** Are you _____ on Monday at three-fifteen?

  B I'm _____ Monday is no _____ .

3. **A** This is Sam at Health Associates. I want to remind you about your appointment tomorrow.

  B Unfortunately, I am _____ to make my appointment. Can I _____ it?

4. **A** We have an _____ on Tuesday at two o'clock.

  B Tuesday at two o'clock _____ for me.

Speak Out | Pair Work

Find a partner. Then, role-play the situations by using the expressions above. Take turns being a patient and a receptionist.

Making an Appointment	Cancelling an Appointment
A Hi. My name is (your name). I have a (medical problem.) I'd like to make a doctor's appointment. **B** (Availability) **A** (Say you are available.)	**A** This is (your name). I'm calling to remind you about your appointment (day and time). **B** (Cancel the appointment.)

Conversation ❸ *Visiting the ER*

A If you go to the emergency room in the United States, you will be asked to fill out some paperwork related to your health insurance status, your medical history, and other important information. Depending on your condition, you may have to wait a while to see a doctor. Listen and practice the conversation with a partner.

Lina is visiting the ER because she sprained her ankle.

Lina	*(limping)* Hi. I'd like to see a doctor.
Receptionist	Have you visited our hospital before?
Lina	No, this is my first time.
Receptionist	What's the problem?
Lina	I sprained my ankle while going for a run.
Receptionist	Do you have health insurance?
Lina	Yes, I do. I'm covered by Life Partners.
Receptionist	I'd like you to fill out some paperwork first.
Lina	What kind of paperwork?
Receptionist	Since this is your first time here, we need your name, insurance information, and medical history.
Lina	Will it take a long time to see a doctor?
Receptionist	We're a little busy this morning, so it might be a little while before a doctor can see you. The doctors need to tend to the most critical patients first.
Lina	Okay, I understand.
Receptionist	Please complete the forms on this clipboard and return them to me when you're done. You can take a seat in our waiting room.
Lina	Great, thank you. I will.

⊘ **Words to Know** sprain ankle paperwork critical

B Practice the conversation with a partner. Use the information in the box below.

A I'd like you to ¹ .... some paperwork first.

B What kind of ² .... ?

A Since this is your first time here, we need your name, insurance information, and ³ ....

1	2	3
complete	information do you want	medical information
finish	forms should I complete	medical past
do	paperwork is it	previous medical conditions

Language Focus

Look at the sample of the emergency room admittance form. Then, match the information in the box to the correct spaces on the form.

ⓐ type 1 diabetes   ⓑ 312-2959-4957   ⓒ 01.25.1999
ⓓ Life Partners   ⓔ Dayeon Hong   ⓕ sprained ankle

Emergency Room Admittance Form

Name: [1]

DOB: [2]

Social Security # / Passport #: M349459929

Address: 4839 Park Place, Los Angeles, CA

Phone #: 323-4949-2356

Health Insurance Carrier:
[4]

Health Insurance Number:
4838302002018

Allergies to Medicines:

None

Emergency Contact
Name: Paul Pittman
Phone Number: [5]

Reason for ER Visit Today:

[3]

Current and Past Medical Issues:

[6]

Speak Out | Pair Work

Find a partner. Then, fill out the form with your partner's information by asking him or her questions related to the information on the emergency room admittance form.

Emergency Room Admittance Form

Name:

DOB:

Social Security # / Passport #:

Address:

Phone #:

Health Insurance Carrier:

Health Insurance Number:

Allergies to Medicines:

Emergency Contact
Name:
Phone Number:

Reason for ER Visit Today:

Current and Past Medical Issues:

Wrap It Up

Vocabulary Check — Complete the sentences by using the words in the box.

cancellation	sprained	diagnosed	hoarse	opening

1. Jane was _____ with a bad lung infection.
2. The clinic has a 24-hour _____ policy. Failure to do so 24 hours before your appointment will result in a $100 fee.
3. Jacob's voice is _____ from cheering for his favorite basketball team, the Clippers.
4. I _____ my ankle on my way to class this morning.
5. Do you happen to have an _____ this afternoon?

Situation Talk

A Write down four medical symptoms in the chart. Then, tell your partner you are suffering from the symptoms. Ask your partner what you should do. Write down your partner's advice in the chart.

Symptoms	Partner's Advice

B Role-play the following situation with a partner.

 Role A

You are calling to make a doctor's appointment.

1. Tell B that you would like to make an appointment.
2. Tell B that you are suffering from indigestion.
3. Say you're not available in the morning that day. Ask if there is an opening in the afternoon.
4. Tell B that 5 p.m. works for you. Say thank you.

 Role B

You are a receptionist at the local clinic.

1. Ask B what the problem is.
2. Say okay. Tell A that Dr. Kim has an opening on March 10 at 11 a.m.
3. Tell A that there is an opening at 5 p.m.
4. Tell A that he or she is welcome.

Preventative Care

Track 35

It is common knowledge around the world that the American diet is not a healthy one. Fast food and sugary drinks have become a staple of the American diet, much to the detriment of people's health. Much of the health care in America centers around treating preventable illnesses such as high blood pressure, high cholesterol, and type 2 diabetes. These ailments, along with many others, can be controlled or eradicated by eating healthfully and by exercising regularly.

Some medical experts in the United States are beginning to encourage good preventative care in order to help patients avoid diseases and eventual hospitalizations later. For example, a diet in which there is a healthy balance of fat, protein, and carbohydrates would eliminate the need for many Americans to take blood pressure-lowering or cholesterol-lowering medications. These health issues are most often the direct results of diets rich in starchy and sugary foods such as potato chips and donuts.

Aside from diet, exercise is also one of the ways Americans can practice good preventative care. Lifting weights, even light weights for injured or older people, can reduce the onset of osteoporosis. By building thicker, denser bone mass through exercise, Americans can reduce the occurrence of bone breaks which often result in long hospitalizations and other complications later in life. Aerobic exercise can make the heart and the lungs healthier and stronger. This can reduce the incidence of strokes and heart attacks. Therapy for strokes can be very expensive and perhaps impossible to receive if a patient is uninsured. Bypass surgery for heart attack victims is also extremely expensive and requires a long recovery period. In all, good preventative care such as eating right and getting regular exercise can eliminate much of the medical care needs that now exist in the United States.

Read the article. Check T for true or F for false.

1. The typical American diet is high in protein and fat.   T ☐ / F ☐
2. Weightlifting can delay or eliminate the onset of osteoporosis. T ☐ / F ☐
3. Aerobic exercise can reduce the occurrence of strokes and heart attacks. T ☐ / F ☐

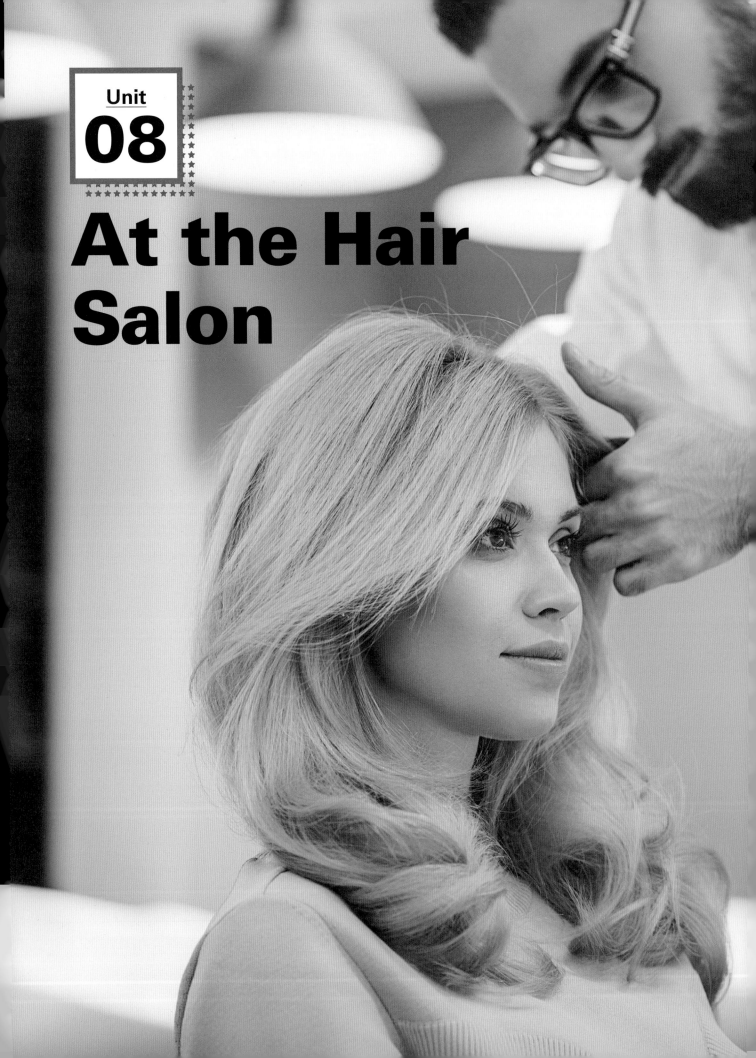

Unit 08
At the Hair Salon

Discuss the following questions.

1. How often do you get your hair cut?
2. How much do you usually spend at the hair salon?
3. Do you go to a particular hair salon? Do you usually make an appointment with your hairdresser?

Track 36

Barber Shops and Hair Salons

Fifty years ago, in the United States, men went to the barber shop, and women went to the hair salon. It would have been considered strange for a man to get his hair cut at a hair salon. That was where women had their hair cut, trimmed, permed, and straightened. The barber shop was a manly place where men had their hair cut by a male barber and read men's magazines like *Playboy* while waiting their turn. And there was not much of a variety of hairstyles available for men back then. Barbers knew how to give someone a trim, a shave, or a buzzcut, but overall, they did not offer much variety when it came to different hairstyles.

Over time, barber shops began to disappear as hair salons became more prominent. In the 80s and 90s, it felt as if every mini-mall in the country had a hair salon in it. By then, it had become acceptable for American men to adopt a wider range of hairstyles, ones the previous generation considered feminine. Eventually, the hair salon became the place where both men and women had their hair done. It also became much more common to see male hairdressers cutting both men's and women's hair. What we really have nowadays is a merging of the two, the hair salon and the barber shop, into one.

Conversation ❶ *Making an Appointment with My Hairdresser*

Track 37

A Popular hairdressers are vigorously sought by clients. Because of this, clients have to make appointments with their hairdressers. Not all hairdressers insist on appointments, but the most talented ones do. You have to remember that the best hairdressers are the most expensive, too. This is a conversation between a woman and her hairdresser. Listen and practice the conversation with a partner.

Lily is making a hair appointment with Phillipe, her hairdresser.

Phillipe Hey, Lily! Are you calling to make an appointment?

Lily That's right.

Phillipe How's next Monday at 1:00 p.m.?

Lily No good. I have a meeting then. How about Tuesday at 1:00?

Phillipe Sorry. I have another client already booked then.

Lily Hmm. Do you have anyone on Wednesday?

Phillipe Nope.

Lily 1:00 p.m. on Wednesday it is then.

Phillipe Do you want the same as the last time: a cut and coloring?

Lily I'm thinking about a perm. What do you think?

Phillipe You have such a pretty face, Lily. I think it would draw attention away from it. Did you see Charlize Theron's haircut at this year's Academy Awards?

Lily Yes, I did. I loved it on her, but do you think I can pull it off?

Phillipe You're beautiful! Of course, you can.

Lily Okay, I trust you Phillipe.

✅**Words to Know** client draw attention away from pull it off trust

B Practice the conversation with a partner. Use the information in the box below.

A I'm thinking about ¹ _____ . What do you think?

B You have such ² _____ . I think it would draw attention away from that fact. Did you see ³ _____ new haircut at this year's Academy Awards?

A Yes, I did. I loved it on her, but do you think I can pull it off?

B You're beautiful! Of course, you can.

1	2	3
coloring my hair	lovely brown eyes	Natalie Portman's
bangs	piercing blue eyes	Renee Zellweger's
cutting my hair short	a pretty face	Scarlett Johansson's

Language Focus

A There are a lot of vocabulary words related to getting your hair done that will be useful while staying in the United States. Look at the chart.

People	Hair		Hair Products	
Hi. I'll be your _____.	*I'd like* _____.		*Can I get some* _____?	
• barber	• a haircut	• a perm	• gel	• mousse
• hair stylist	• a wash	• a blow-dry	• wax	• hairspray
• hairdresser	• to color my hair	• highlights	• shampoo	• conditioner
	• a trim	• scalp care		

B Match the sentences with the correct pictures.

ⓐ I'd like a **perm**.
ⓒ Please put some **mousse** on top.
ⓔ Would you like some **wax** in your hair?
ⓑ Can you **blow-dry** it?
ⓓ I'm here to get a **haircut**.
ⓕ I'd like a **wash** first.

Speak Out | Pair Work

Find a partner. Then, role-play the situations by using the vocabulary above. Take turns being a customer and a hairdresser.

Hair	Hair Products
A HI. I'll be your (hairdresser). How can I help you? **B** I'd like (a haircut). **A** Would you like me to wash your hair first? **B** Yes, I would.	**A** I'm finished. What kind of product would you like in your hair? **B** Can I get some (wax)? **A** Okay. All done. **B** Thank you!

Conversation ② *Walk-ins*

A There are some common terms hairdressers use with customers in order to get the exact looks they are seeking. If you do not understand a term the hairdresser uses, just ask him or her to explain the meaning. He or she will happily assist you. Listen and practice the conversation with a partner.

Francisco is asking the manager at a hair salon if the establishment accepts walk-ins.

Francisco	Do you accept walk-ins?
Manager	Yes, we do. I think Brenda is free.
Francisco	Great.
Manager	Brenda, can you take care of this customer?
Brenda	Of course. *(to Francisco)* Have a seat in the barber's chair.
Francisco	Okay.
Brenda	How would you like me to cut your hair today?
Francisco	I'd like it short on the sides and back.
Brenda	Do you want it faded?
Francisco	No. I just want it cut short on the back and sides, but not shaved.
Brenda	Okay, I understand. How about the top?
Francisco	I'm thinking about growing it out.
Brenda	Would you like me to layer it, so it grows out more neatly?
Francisco	Yes, that's exactly what I want.
Brenda	Great. Let's get your hair washed and blow-dried before we cut it.

⊘ **Words to Know**   accept   walk-in   faded   blow-dry

B Practice the conversation with a partner. Use the information in the box below.

A How would you like me to cut your hair today?

B I'd like it ¹ _____ on the ² _____ .

A Do you want ³ _____ ?

B Yes, that's exactly what I want.

1	2	3
really short	sides and back	me to use clippers
tapered	sides	it faded
long on the sides, the back, and	top	me to layer it

Language Focus

A There are several expressions you can use when advising your hairdresser about the hairstyle you are interested in getting. Look at the chart.

Haircut	Perm / Dyeing
I'd like my head shaved. / I want it shaved on the sides.	I would like to get my hair permed.
I want you to layer it on the sides and leave it a little long on top.	I want to get a wavy/curly perm.
Can you cut my hair to my shoulders?	I want it straightened.
I'd like to get bangs.	I'd like my hair colored.

B Look at the pictures and complete the conversations by using the words in the box.

 1.  2.  3.  4.

1. A How would you like your hair done?

   B I'd like my hair _____ .

2. A How would you like me to cut your hair?

   B I want it _____ on the sides.

3. A How would you like your hair done today?

   B I want to get a _____ .

4. A How would you like your hair cut?

   B I'd like to get _____ .

shaved	bangs	colored	curly perm

Speak Out | Pair Work

Find a partner. Then, imagine your partner is getting a haircut, and you are the hairdresser. Ask your partner how he or she likes his or her hair cut. Draw hair on the people's heads below which matches the style your partner prefers. After that, switch roles.

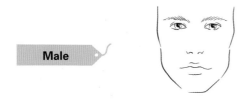 Male

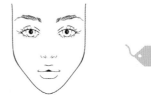 Female

A *How would you like your hair done today?*

B *Make it short on the sides and back, please.*

Conversation ③ *At the Beauty Salon*

Track 39

A America also has places called beauty salons which extend services beyond hair to include things such as skin care, facial care, pedicures, manicures, and aromatherapy. Many women as well as men enjoy going to the beauty salon as a form of relaxation therapy. Listen and practice the conversation with a partner.

Jeongah received a $200 gift card for a beauty salon in her city. She is asking the receptionist some questions regarding use of the gift card.

Receptionist	Welcome to Health 'n' Wellness Beauty Salon!
Jeongah	Hi. I have a gift card for your beauty salon, but I'm not sure which services it is good for.
Receptionist	May I see the card?
Jeongah	Here you are.
Receptionist	This is our Rose Gift Card. It's good for a haircut, a mani/pedi, and your choice of facial treatment or aromatherapy.
Jeongah	I'm sorry, but what is a mani/pedi?
Receptionist	Oh, I'm sorry. Mani stands for manicure or nail care, and pedi stands for pedicure, which is foot care.
Jeongah	Oh, I see. And I have to choose facial treatment or aromatherapy?
Receptionist	Yes, that's right.
Jeongah	I'd like the facial treatment.
Receptionist	No problem. Let me bring Cathy over here. She'll be taking care of you today.

⊘ **Words to Know**   gift card   good for   treatment   stand for

B Practice the conversation with a partner. Use the information in the box below.

A Hi. I have a ¹ _____ for your beauty salon, but I'm not sure which services it is good for.

B May I see it?

A Here you are.

B This is our Rose Gift Card. It's good for a haircut, ² _____ , and ³ _____ .

1	2	3
gift certificate	a facial	a pedicure
gift voucher	a manicure	aromatherapy
gift card	a mani	a pedi

Language Focus

There are several kinds of services available at beauty salons that extend beyond the traditional services you will find at a hair salon. These services make excellent gifts, and gift vouchers can often be purchased at these places and given to friends and family as presents. Match the types of services at beauty salons to the correct pictures.

aromatherapy   facial   manicure   massage   pedicure   waxing

1.

2.

3.

4.

5.

6.

Speak Out | Class Activity

Complete the "Have you ever ...?" activity by asking students in your class the questions. Write down the person's name if he or she says yes. If he or she says yes, ask a follow-up question related to the first question.

Have you ever ...?	Name	More Information
had aromatherapy		
had a manicure		
had a pedicure		
had facial treatment		
had a professional massage		

A *Have you ever had aromatherapy?*
B *Yes. I've had it several times.*
A *How did you like it?*
B *I felt relaxed.*

Vocabulary Check Match the words with their correct definitions.

1. walk-in •
2. trust •
3. pull it off •
4. gift card •
5. blow-dry •

• ⓐ to enter a hair salon without an appointment

• ⓑ to successfully do something

• ⓒ to dry your hair with a hairdryer

• ⓓ to believe in something or someone

• ⓔ a card given to someone as a present for goods or services from the issuer; the same as a voucher

Situation Talk

A **Find a partner. Then, imagine he or she is your hairdresser. Explain how you like your hair to be done. Switch roles.**

B **Role-play the following situation with a partner.**

Role **A**	Role **B**
You have a gift card for a beauty salon.	*You are a receptionist at a beauty salon.*
1. Greet B. Say you have a $200 gift card for his or her beauty salon. Ask B which services your gift card provides. 2. Give the gift card to B. 3. Tell B that you prefer a massage.	1. Greet A. Ask A to let you see the gift card. 2. Tell A that he or she can get a haircut, a manicure, a pedicure, and a massage or a waxing with this card. 3. Introduce A to Kaitlin, his or her masseuse.

C **Find a partner. Then, discuss the following questions with him or her.**

1. What's the worst haircut you have ever had? Who gave it to you? How old were you?

2. What's the best haircut you have ever had? Who gave it to you? How old were you?

3. Who usually cuts your hair? Why do you like him or her?

4. Do you perm, dye, or straighten your hair? If so, how often do you get it done?

5. How do you like your hair cut: long, short, layered, faded, shaved, etc.?

The Crazy History of the Barber Shop

Track 40

The crazy history of the barber shop is fascinating and provides some insight into how difficult life was for the European peasantry during the Middle Ages. Unbeknownst to many, barbers during the Middle Ages did not simply provide men with haircuts and shaves. For many people in the underclass, they were surgeons and dentists, too. For example, if a poor person during the Middle Ages needed a tooth pulled, he or she would go to the local barber because the local physician was too expensive. Physicians worked for the aristocracy, or the upper class. You can just imagine how awful, and potentially dangerous, an operation like that would have been in those times.

Another procedure, one which is no longer practiced, is bloodletting. People believed illnesses and diseases could be bled out. The idea was that the illness or disease stemmed from bad blood, and if that bad blood could be removed from the body, the patient could recover. Oftentimes, people succumbed to their illnesses or diseases because of this bad practice, one which also had no medical usefulness. It was the bloodletting, though, that inspired the creation of the barber pole.

Traditional barber poles contain only two colors: red and white. The red signifies the blood in a bloodletting procedure, and the white signifies the handkerchief or bandage which was wrapped around the wound. The pole was inspired by the poles that patients were encouraged to hold onto while they were being bled. Later versions of the pole contained a blue stripe, which historians believe represented the blue in the American flag for barber shops in the United States. In Europe, the blue provided a distinction between barbers and surgeons. It is hard to believe that barber poles represent such a barbaric history. I bet you will never look at a barber pole the same way again!

Read the article. Answer these questions.
1. Aside from cutting hair, what other services did barbers provide in the Middle Ages?
2. What procedure was common during the Middle Ages but is no longer practiced these days?
3. What do the red and white stripes in a barber pole represent?

Unit 09

Professional Life

Discuss the following questions.

1. Do you enjoy working in an office? What are the good and bad points?
2. Is there a dress code at your workplace or university? If so, what is it?
3. What was your first job interview like? How did it go?

Work Experience on Your Résumé

In America, it is not uncommon for job applicants to list their part-time work experience on their résumés, especially when they do not have a lot of experience to begin with. The reason people in the United States do this is to show their potential employers that they have ambition and choose to work, even in menial jobs, wherever and whenever it is possible.

In countries such as Korea, it would be inappropriate to put a small part-time job on one's résumé because it would not be considered serious work, and would diminish the quality of the résumé. The opposite is true in the USA. An American employer would not look down on an applicant for listing his or her work at Starbucks or McDonald's. The fact that the person was willing to do work that was below his or her educational level shows chutzpah, a Yiddish word meaning audacity or willingness to take risks. American companies like this quality in a job applicant.

If you are applying for a job in the United States and you have recently graduated from university, it is best to list some kind of work experience on your résumé. The potential employer wants to know that you can accept a job, any job, hold on to that job, and fulfill your commitment to that employer by not immediately leaving the job. By showing that you worked in high school or college, you can show your potential employer that you are a serious person and that you are willing to stay with a job even if things get difficult at times.

Conversation ① *A Job Interview*

Track 42

A When interviewing for a job, it is best to be a little early but not too early. When you are called upon to interview for a job, remember to smile. Be friendly but also serious. Most of all, just be honest with your answers. If you try to oversell yourself, the interviewer will notice. This is a conversation between a job applicant and a job interviewer. Listen and practice the conversation with a partner.

Anna is interviewing for a job at an American company in the United States.

Mr. Simmons Have a seat right there. Now, tell me about yourself.

Anna I'm Korean. I grew up in Korea and moved to the States four years ago for university.

Mr. Simmons Where did you study?

Anna I graduated from UCLA with a double major in business management and communications.

Mr. Simmons Wow. What interesting choices! Would you consider yourself a type A individual or a type B?

Anna I'm definitely more of a type A person. I'm extremely organized—almost too organized. And I am obsessed with being on time. My friends say I'm an overachiever.

Mr. Simmons Those are all good qualities in my opinion. I'm also type A. So, what kind of work experience do you have?

Anna I have been a waitress at a bar near my school for the past three years. I have a recommendation from my manager.

Mr. Simmons Great. Is that recommendation in the packet with your résumé and cover letter?

Anna Yes, it is.

⊘ **Words to Know** major organized obsessed recommendation

B Practice the conversation with a partner. Use the information in the box below.

A Have a seat right there. Now, tell me about yourself.

B I grew up in ¹ _____ and moved to the States four years ago for university.

A Where did you study?

B I graduated from ² _____ with a double major in business management and ³ _____ .

1	2	3
China	Ohio State University	accounting
Japan	Ithaca College	marketing
Thailand	Northwestern University	statistics

Language Focus

A Most interviewers will ask you to tell him or her about yourself at some point during the interview. When an interviewer asks you to describe youself, it is best to have a prepared answer to the question. You want to be honest, but you also want to frame the answer in a positive way. Look at some sample answers in the chart.

Talking about Yourself	
Where are you from? (background)	**What are you like? (personality)**
I was born in New York.	I'm friendly and creative.
I come from a small village in Italy.	I'm an organized person.
I am from Korea.	I have a type A personality. (organized, ambitious, punctual)
My home country is Canada.	I have a type B personality. (flexible, relaxed, empathetic)
I grew up in London.	I like to think outside the box.

B Read the sentences and check which one you think is the most appropriate: a type A personality or a type B personality.

1. I like to get to work about ten minutes early. Type A ☐ Type B ☐

2. I like to think outside the box. Type A ☐ Type B ☐

3. I'm a creative person. I'm good at brainstorming ideas. Type A ☐ Type B ☐

4. Once I start a task, I must finish it. Type A ☐ Type B ☐

5. I keep the files on my computer desktop organized alphabetically. Type A ☐ Type B ☐

6. I never get stressed out, even in stressful situations. Type A ☐ Type B ☐

Speak Out | Pair Work

Find a partner. Then, ask your partner to tell you about himself or herself. When you are finished, decide if your partner has a type A personality or a type B personality. Switch roles.

Conversation ② *Office Etiquette*

A **Nothing poisons the atmosphere in an office like gossip. Gossip has a tendency to travel around, and eventually, the person that is being gossiped about finds out. It can not only lead to strained relationships, but it can put your job at risk. This is a conversation between two coworkers in an office. Listen and practice the conversation with a partner.**

Praya is talking to her colleague, Dan, in an office.

Dan Hey, Praya. Did you get my email?

Praya Yeah. Thanks.

Dan No problem. The manager asked me to send the email to everyone in the accounting department.

Praya Okay.

Dan He always asks me to send emails. It's getting really annoying.

Praya I'm actually really busy …

Dan And he's so stupid! Anyone could do his job, even the interns.

Praya I'm sorry, Dan, but I don't have time for …

Dan Don't you hate him? He really puts a lot of pressure on the staff. I know at least three people in this office that can't stand him.

Praya I've never had a problem with Mr. West.

Dan Come on, Praya. You can't tell me that you actually like that guy.

Praya Look, Dan. I really don't have time for this right now. It's bad etiquette to gossip about people behind their backs. If you have a problem with Mr. West, you should talk to him about it.

Dan Whatever.

⊘**Words to Know** annoying intern pressure gossip

B **Practice the conversation with a partner. Use the information in the box below.**

A He's so ¹ _____ ! Anyone could do his job, even the interns.

B I'm sorry, Dan, but I don't have time for ...

A ² _____ ? He really puts a lot of pressure on the staff. I know at least three people in this office that can't stand him.

B ³ _____ with Mr. West.

1	2	3
dumb	Doesn't he bother you	I haven't got any problems
ignorant	Doesn't he annoy you	I don't have any problems
unintelligent	Don't you hate him	I don't have any beefs

Language Focus

Good office etiquette is very important in the United States. Here are several bad behaviors that can cause conflict and problems in offices. Look at the behaviors in the word box and match them with the correct pictures.

ⓐ not listening during meetings
ⓑ using foul language
ⓒ working while sick
ⓓ interrupting people
ⓔ complaining
ⓕ speaking too loudly
ⓖ gossiping
ⓗ eating smelly food at your desk
ⓘ having bad hygiene

1.

2.

3.

4.

5.

6.

7.

8.

S#*T!

9.

Speak Out | Pair Work

Find a partner. Then, rank the bad behaviors above from 1, the most offensive, to 9, the least offensive.

1		4		7	
2		5		8	
3		6		9	

Conversation ③ *Giving Two Weeks' Notice*

⊙ Track **44**

A In America, it is good etiquette to provide your company with two weeks' notice when leaving your position. This gives the company a suitable amount of time to find a replacement and to give that replacement adequate training. This is a conversation between a boss and an employee who has given her two weeks' notice. Listen and practice the conversation with a partner.

Praya is giving her two weeks' notice to Mr. West.

Mr. West Praya, I just wanted to pop in and say you did a great job on the Johnson report.

Praya Thank you, Mr. West. Actually, I really want to talk to you about something.

Mr. West Of course. What is it?

Praya First of all, I just want you to know that I have really enjoyed my time here and that I have learned so much.

Mr. West We really enjoy having you as part of our accounting team.

Praya Unfortunately, I have to give you my two weeks' notice. My parents own a small accounting firm in Bangkok, Thailand, and they want me to come back and work for them.

Mr. West I'd be lying if I said I wasn't disappointed with the news, but I appreciate that you are giving me sufficient notice to find a replacement.

Praya Of course, I will submit a formal resignation this afternoon.

Mr. West You can give it to Dan, my assistant. He handles all resignation letters. We're really going to miss you. You have done a great job here. If you ever find yourself back in Chicago, give me a call. I'll hire you in a second!

⊘ **Words to Know** two weeks' notice   pop in   firm   resignation letter

B Practice the conversation with a partner. Use the information in the box below.

A Unfortunately, I have to give you my two weeks' notice. My parents own a small ¹_____ firm in Bangkok, Thailand, and they want me to come back and work for them.

B I'd be lying if I said I wasn't disappointed with the news, but I appreciate that you are giving me ²_____ notice to find a replacement.

A Of course, I will ³_____ a formal resignation letter this afternoon.

B You can give it to Dan, my assistant. He handles all resignation letters.

1	2	3
marketing	sufficient	give you
advertising	advance	turn in
graphic design	two weeks'	hand you

Language Focus

A There are actually three different pronunciations for regular verbs in the past simple tense in English. They are all spelled by using an -ed at the end of the verb; however, they have three distinct sound endings. Look at the chart and read the words aloud.

Pronunciation of -ed		
/d/	**/t/**	**/ɪd/**
• enjoy**ed**	• walk**ed**	• want**ed**
• learn**ed**	• help**ed**	• disappoint**ed**
• call**ed**	• reach**ed**	• decid**ed**
• lov**ed**	• guess**ed**	• contact**ed**
• claim**ed**	• laugh**ed**	• add**ed**

B Put the regular past simple tense verbs in the box into their correct categories.

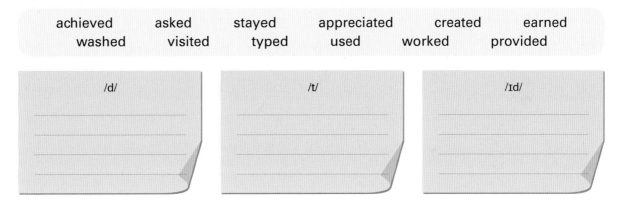

achieved　　asked　　stayed　　appreciated　　created　　earned

washed　　visited　　typed　　used　　worked　　provided

/d/	/t/	/ɪd/

Speak Out | Pair Work

Find a partner. Then, perform five clear actions in front of your partner. (For example, open your book.) When you have completed five actions, have your partner recite the five actions to you aloud by using the past simple tense. Switch roles.

*First, you **opened** your book.*
*Next, you **picked up** your pencil and set it down.*
*After that, you **clapped** your hands five times.*
*Then, you **stretched** your arms.*
*Finally, you **pretended** to sleep at your desk.*

Wrap It Up

Vocabulary Check — Fill in the blanks with the correct answers.

1. Sumin is _____ with being on time. She's never late.

    ⓐ organized   ⓑ obsessed

2. Do you mind if I _____ for a visit after class?   ⓐ pop in   ⓑ firm

3. What was your _____ in university?   ⓐ major   ⓑ recommendation

4. He is under a lot of _____ at work these days.   ⓐ gossip   ⓑ pressure

5. She submitted her _____, taking responsibility for the incident.

    ⓐ resignation letter   ⓑ two weeks' notice

Situation Talk

A   **Role-play the following situation with a partner.**

Role **A**	Role **B**
You are interviewing B, a job applicant.	*You are interviewing for a job at A's company.*
1. Greet B. Ask B to take a seat. 2. Ask B to tell him or her about himself or herself. 3. Ask B what his or her major is. 4. Tell B that his or her résumé is very impressive. 5. Ask B what his or her personality is like.	1. Greet A. Say okay. 2. Say where you are from. Say that you went to college in the United States and that you have just graduated. 3. Tell A that you have a double-major. Say that you majored in economics and business administration. 4. Say thank you. 5. Say what you are like.

B   **Find a partner. Then, ask your partner the questions below. Let your partner answer the questions by using the correct pronunciations of the regular verbs in the past simple tense.**

1. What did you **want** to be when you were a child?

2. Who did you **call** most recently? How long did you **talk**?

3. Which sports did you **play** in elementary, middle, and high school?

4. Which classmate did you first **talk** to in today's class?

5. Where did you **decide** to sit in the classroom today?

6. When did you last **visit** your grandparents?

A   *What did you **want** to be when you were a child?*

B   *I **wanted** to be a police officer.*

What Should I Wear?

These days, appropriate work attire is not as simple as it was in the past. In the past, men wore suits to the office, and women wore conservative suits with coordinating blouses. Of course, nice leather shoes, belts, and conservative haircuts and hairstyles were also expected. In the era of Internet startups and casual Fridays, things have become more complicated. Here are some quick and dirty tips if you are confused about what to wear to that job interview or on your first day of work.

1. If interviewing for a job, men should always show up in a dark suit, including leather shoes, a nice belt, an appropriate tie, and a conservative hairstyle. Women should wear a suit (pants or a skirt are both acceptable), a coordinating blouse, leather shoes, and a conservative hairstyle. Anything other than this kind of attire for a job interview would be inappropriate in professional America. Even if the workplace environment is casual, you want to show the interviewer that you are a serious person and take the position you are applying for very seriously.

2. In the workplace, you need to pay attention to the corporate culture. If you show up for your interview in a suit, and the interviewer shows up in jeans, a T-shirt, and sneakers, do not worry. You can make adjustments on your first day in the office. If you end up getting the job you are applying for, do not be afraid to ask about appropriate work attire. You may find that on the day you were interviewed, the company was having a casual Friday. You would not want to show up wearing jeans on your first day when everyone else is wearing a suit.

3. What is the difference between business formal, business casual, and casual? Business formal means you are wearing a suit, a dress shirt, leather shoes, a leather belt, and a tie. Business casual does not mean that you can wear jeans. Cotton pants with a dark polo shirt or dress shirt is appropriate business casual attire. If you are lucky enough to work for a company that has a casual dress code, then jeans, T-shirts, and hoodies are okay, but make sure there are no rips or tears in your clothes. You still want to make a good impression and to be taken seriously even if the corporate culture is casual.

Read the article. Check T for true or F for false.
1. It is okay to wear cotton pants and a polo shirt to an interview sometimes. T ☐ / F ☐
2. It is okay to ask someone at the company about appropriate work attire. T ☐ / F ☐
3. A casual work environment means it is okay to wear ripped jeans. T ☐ / F ☐

Weddings

ⓝ Track **46**

Great Wedding or Great Marriage?

Given the dire financial situations of many individuals from the Millennial generation, large numbers of young people from this demographic are abandoning the idea of marriage altogether. For those lucky enough to scrape the money together for a wedding, the $30,000 average bill often leaves them in a perilous financial situation once the "I dos" have been said. The day after the wedding, mortgage or rental payments have to be made, furniture has to be purchased, and decisions regarding starting a family have to be made. This reality often leaves these young people with a terrible choice: to have a great wedding or to have a great marriage.

The first year of marriage is difficult enough without the added burden of wedding debt. One of the leading causes of divorce in the United States is disagreements over money. The truth is that weddings are just too darn expensive. In the United States, we have an expression: "Keeping up with the Jones's." It speaks about the human impulse to always one-up your neighbor. If your friend has an amazing wedding, then the pressure for your wedding to be even better is profound. And the only way to outdo the previous wedding is to spend more money. Every bride and groom want to feel like Cinderella and Prince Charming, but does it not make more sense to scale down the wedding and to scale up the actual marriage? I mean, one will last a single day, but the other, hopefully, will last a lifetime.

Discuss the following questions.

1. Are you married? If so, what was your wedding like? If not, would you like to get married?
2. Have you ever been to a wedding? What was it like?
3. How much does the average wedding cost in your country?

Conversation 1 An Invitation to Be a Maid of Honor

◉ Track 47

A When a couple decides to get married in the United States, the man will ask his best friend to be his best man, and the woman will ask her best friend to be her maid of honor. There are a number of duties that the best man and the maid of honor are responsible for. In this conversation, a woman is asking her best friend to be the maid of honor at her wedding. Listen and practice the conversation with a partner.

Caroline is asking Suhyeon to be her maid of honor.

Caroline I have to ask you something really important, Suhyeon.

Suhyeon Is everything okay?

Caroline Everything's perfect.

Suhyeon Oh, my gosh! Did Andrew propose?

Caroline Yes!

Suhyeon *(screaming)* That's amazing! Congratulations! Let me see the ring.

Caroline It's right here. Isn't it beautiful?

Suhyeon It is. And Andrew is such a sweet guy. I'm so happy for you.

Caroline I asked you to come over because I wanted to ask you something really important.

Suhyeon What is it?

Caroline Will you be my maid of honor?

Suhyeon I'd be honored, but what do I have to do?

Caroline You'll stand next to me at the wedding ceremony. And traditionally, the maid of honor organizes a bachelorette party.

Suhyeon Okay. I'm throwing you the best bachelorette party you've ever seen!

⊘ **Words to Know**   maid of honor   propose   bachelorette party

B Practice the conversation with a partner. Use the information in the box below.

A Will you be ¹ _____ ?

B I'd be honored, but what do I have to do?

A You'll stand next to me at the wedding ceremony. And traditionally, you ² _____ a

³ _____ .

B It's going to be the best party you've ever seen!

1	2	3
my best man	throw me	bachelor party
my maid of honor	give me	bachelorette party
my bridesmaid	arrange	bridal shower

Language Focus

A We can use the modal auxiliary verb *will* and the phrase *be going to* to talk about future plans in English, but native English speakers also use the present continuous tense to talk about future plans as well. Look at the chart.

Happening Now	A Plan for the Future
I'm **having** a great time at the bachelor party. I'm **driving** right now. I'll call you later. We're **staying** at the Hudson Hotel now. He's **practicing** the guitar at the moment.	I'm **throwing** you the best bachelor party ever! We're **doing** another round of shots when this song is finished. We're **having** breakfast at 9:00 a.m. tomorrow. They're **playing** soccer tomorrow morning.

B Write "N" if the sentence means it is happening now or "F" if it will take place in the future.

1. Look! Alex **is dancing** with Jessica. Jessica's boyfriend is going to be angry. ☐

2. We're **going** to Hawaii for our summer vacation. ☐

3. Jin **is getting** married to Beth on Saturday. ☐

4. I'm **calling** Sarah now, but she isn't answering her phone. ☐

5. Hurry up! Jun and Subin **are getting** into the limo. Let's say goodbye. ☐

6. What **are** you **buying** Jake and Michelle for their wedding? ☐

Speak Out | Group Work

Make a group of four or five students. Imagine you are bridesmaids or groomsmen for a friend's wedding. You have been tasked with planning a bachelorette or bachelor party. Complete the chart below with information about your plans for the party. Finally, share your plans for the party with the class.

The Bachelorette/Bachelor Party Night	
Who is coming to the party?	
When are you meeting?	
Where are you going?	
What are you doing there?	

The groomsmen and some college friends of the groom are coming to the party. We are meeting at John's house this Friday evening. We are drinking beer and playing cards until about 10:00 p.m. ...

Conversation ② *Searching a Wedding Registry*

A At American weddings, it is customary to give the bride and the groom a gift. Couples avoid receiving the same gifts from different guests by creating a wedding registry. They create a wedding registry by choosing a local retailer and creating a list of items in that store that they would like guests to purchase for them. When an item is purchased, it is removed from the list. Listen and practice the conversation with a partner.

Junsu and Hyuni are searching an online wedding registry in order to purchase a gift for friends who are getting married.

Junsu What are you doing?

Hyuni I'm looking for a wedding gift for Kevin and Kara. They're registered at Larsen's Department Store.

Junsu What does registered mean?

Hyuni It means they've created an online list of items at Larsen's Department Store that they want their guests to purchase from. That way, they won't get three microwaves on their wedding day.

Junsu Oh, that makes sense. So, what's left on the list?

Hyuni There isn't much left on the list. I see a vase, a rice cooker, and some dinnerware.

Junsu Let's buy them the rice cooker.

Hyuni It's kind of expensive. Do you think we can afford it?

Junsu How much is it?

Hyuni It's $150.

Junsu It's pricey, but they are our good friends after all.

Hyuni Yeah, you're right. And they're having an open bar at the reception.

Junsu There you go. You drive, and I'll drink $150 worth of alcohol.

Hyuni Don't do that. You're too big for me to carry home.

⊘ **Words to Know** register pricey open bar reception

B Practice the conversation with a partner. Use the information in the box below.

A So, what's left on the list?

B There isn't much left on the list. I see a vase, a coffeemaker, and some silverware. That's about it.

A Let's buy them ¹ _____ .

B It's kind of ² _____ . Do you think we ³ _____ ?

1	2	3
the vase	pricey	can afford it
the coffeemaker	cheap	should buy them two things
the silverware	steep	have enough money

104 · BIG POT 2

Language Focus

Household items are common gifts for weddings. Americans think that when a couple gets married, they need items to furnish an empty house. This view is kind of outdated as many couples decide to live together long before they get married. Regardless, it is still customary to buy household items for newlyweds. Look at the pictures of the common household items. Then, match the words to the correct pictures.

| bed linen | dinnerware | espresso machine | blender |
| microwave | iron | pots and pans | vacuum cleaner |

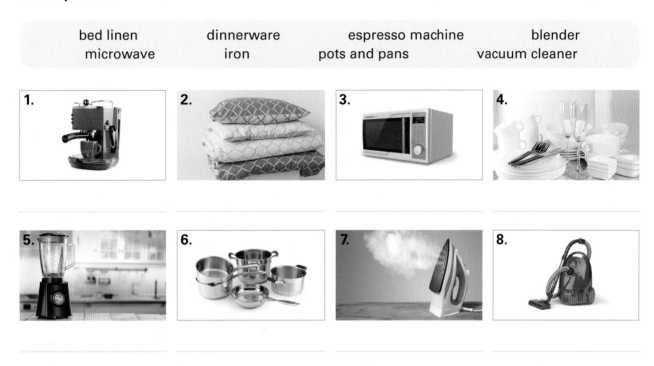

1.

2.

3.

4.

5.

6.

7.

8.

Speak Out | Pair Work

Find a partner. Then, imagine you and your partner are getting married. You are having a small wedding with only 15 guests. Create a wedding registry by making a list of the 15 most important items the two of you will need to begin your lives together. Before you write an item on the list, you must both agree on the item.

_____ and _____ 's Wedding Registry

Conversation ③ *A Wedding DJ*

Track 49

A Wedding receptions often have wedding DJs who play dance music after the wedding dinner is finished. Older guests often leave the wedding reception soon after the dinner; however, younger people tend to stay, drink alcohol, and dance until around midnight. This is a conversation between two guests at a wedding reception. Listen and practice the conversation with a partner.

Jamie and Annabelle are attending a wedding reception as guests.

Jamie	This DJ is awful!
Annabelle	He's not that bad.
Jamie	This is like the tenth slow song in a row.
Annabelle	I think he plays the slow songs first, so the older people can enjoy the music, too.
Jamie	I hadn't thought of that. I want to make a request anyway.
Annabelle	What are you going to request?
Jamie	Something electrifying.
Annabelle	How about some Prince? You could ask him to play *1999*.
Jamie	That's not a bad one. I was thinking about requesting *Celebration* by Kool and the Gang.
Annabelle	That's a great dance song, too.
Jamie	Oh, I've got it. I know the perfect song.
Annabelle	What? What is it?
Jamie	*Crazy* by Gnarls Barkley.
Annabelle	Good call. That'll definitely change the atmosphere in here.
Jamie	I'm going to go talk to the DJ. I'll be back in a sec.
Annabelle	Good luck!

⊘ **Words to Know**   awful   electrifying   good call

B Practice the conversation with a partner. Use the information in the box below.

A What are you going to request?

B Something upbeat. I was thinking about requesting ¹ ....

A ² .... That'll definitely change the ³ .... in here.

1	2	3
Love Shack by the B-52s	Great idea	mood
Last Night by the Strokes	Good thinking	atmosphere
Uptown Funk by Mark Ronson	Great call	feeling

Language Focus

A There are times when we think aloud, especially with close friends and family. One of the ways we do this is by saying "*I was thinking* …". Look at the chart.

I was thinking about/of/that	I was thinking about wearing a suit to the party.
	I was thinking of going there for dinner tonight.
	I was thinking that I would request a song.

B Complete the sentences by using the given words and expressions in the chart.

1. wear / tuxedo   *I was thinking that I would wear a tuxedo.*

2. wear / red dress

3. request / exciting song

4. eat / chicken

5. dance / you

6. drink / cocktail

7. spend the night / hotel

Speak Out | Pair Work

Find a partner. Then, make a list of your top five English language wedding reception dance songs. Do not write down the name of a song until you and your partner both agree. When you are finished with your list, compare it with other pairs in the class.

Our Top 5 Wedding Reception Dance Songs

A *What songs do you think are good for wedding receptions?*
B *How about* We Found Love *by Rihanna?*

Wrap It Up

Vocabulary Check   Complete the sentences by using the words in the box.

propose	electrifying	reception	open bar	awful

1. They've invited a famous band for the _____ .

2. Where did your husband _____ to you?

3. Will there be a cash bar or an _____ at the wedding reception?

4. The weather this summer is _____ . It has been raining for the past three weeks.

5. The mood in here is _____ . I love it!

Situation Talk

A   **Role-play the following situation with a partner.**

Role A	Role B
You are asking your best friend to be the best man / maid of honor at your wedding.	*Your best friend is asking you to be the best man / maid of honor at his or her wedding.*
1. Tell B that there is something important that you have to ask him or her. 2. Tell B that everything is great and you proposed to your girlfriend/boyfriend. 3. Say thank you. Ask B if he or she will be your best man / maid of honor.	1. Ask A if everything is okay. 2. Congratulate A. 3. Tell A that you would be honored to be his or her best man / maid of honor. Say that you are organizing the best bachelor/bachelorette party ever.

B   **Find a partner. Then, imagine you are purchasing a wedding gift for your friends who are getting married. Discuss which item you are going to buy from the wedding registry.**

Blender	Toaster	Cutting Board	Wine Glasses	Teapot	Air Fryer
$39.88	$30.99	$16.99	$24.95	$29.99	$99.99
☐	☐	☐	☐	☐	☐

C   **Make a group of four or five students. Then, discuss the questions about weddings below.**

1. Describe your perfect wedding.

2. Do you want to get married in a church? Why or why not?

3. How do you feel about American wedding receptions? Would you like to have a DJ and a dance at your wedding reception?

4. Is it important for you to have a big wedding? Why or why not?

DIY Weddings vs. Traditional Weddings

Track 50

These days, a growing number of couples are holding smaller, more intimate, do-it-yourself (DIY) wedding ceremonies in backyards and parks across the country. These couples are rejecting the notion that bigger is always better. They are deciding to hold smaller wedding ceremonies where just a few friends and family members are in attendance. These weddings are usually organized by the couples themselves. In turn, couples save tens of thousands of dollars by having friends and family members pitch in with decorations, a cake, food, and photographs. Many of these couples are as satisfied with their DIY weddings as they would have been with lavish church weddings and receptions. Sometimes couples who are marrying for the second or third time decide to hold small weddings in backyards or parks because they have already had the experience of large church weddings. And given that those relationships did not work out, modest weddings with a few close friends and family members are much more attractive to them.

Whether one opts for a wedding with a modest budget or an extravagant wedding ceremony in a church with a nice reception hall, it is important that both the bride and the groom listen to one another. It is quite possible that the bride has been dreaming about her wedding day since she was a young girl. Although the wedding will be expensive, the memory of looking beautiful in a white gown as she is walked down the aisle by her father, like a princess in a fairy tale, is worth every penny to her. Even if the groom is not completely on board with spending that kind of money on the wedding, it is important for him to respect his bride's wishes and try to give her the wedding of her dreams. Sometimes a wedding ceremony in a church is important to a couple for religious purposes. In this case, it is also important for the bride and the groom to follow their hearts and to have the wedding that they have always dreamed of. Although the DIY wedding is not for everybody, it is certainly an alternative that is gaining popularity in these financially difficult times.

Read the article. Answer these questions.
1. What kind of wedding ceremony are a growing number of couples having these days?
2. How can couples save money by having DIY weddings?
3. What should the groom do if the bride has always dreamed of having a large wedding?

Unit 10 · **109**

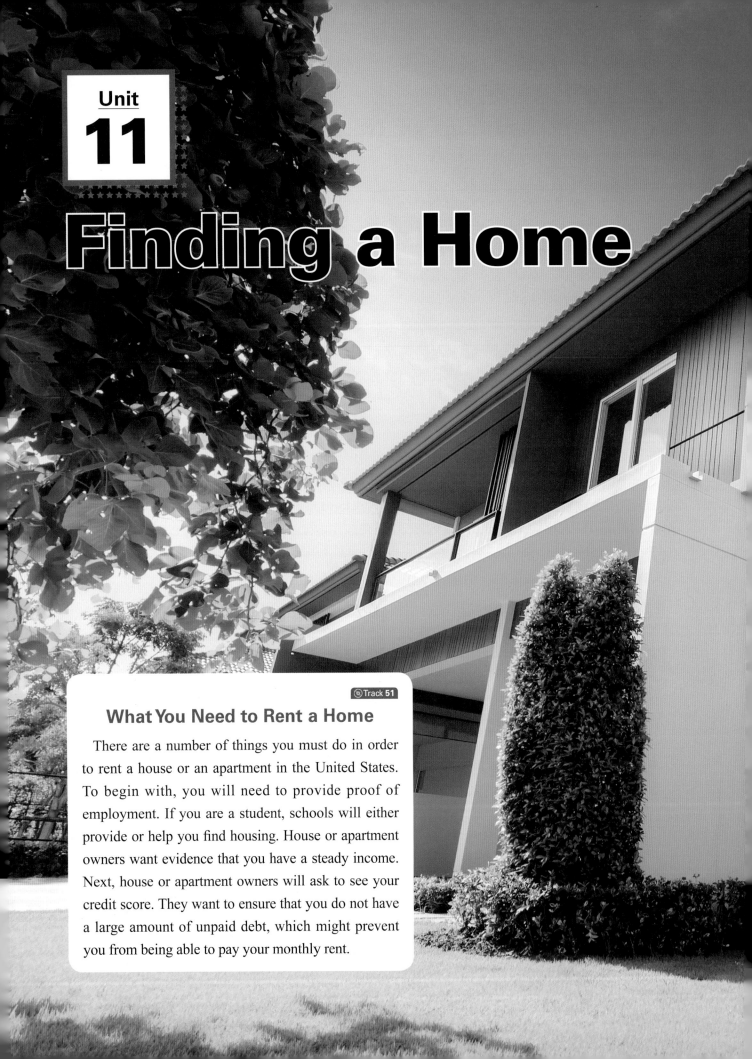

Unit 11

Finding a Home

What You Need to Rent a Home

There are a number of things you must do in order to rent a house or an apartment in the United States. To begin with, you will need to provide proof of employment. If you are a student, schools will either provide or help you find housing. House or apartment owners want evidence that you have a steady income. Next, house or apartment owners will ask to see your credit score. They want to ensure that you do not have a large amount of unpaid debt, which might prevent you from being able to pay your monthly rent.

Discuss the following questions.

1. Have you ever rented a house or an apartment? If so, how did you find it?
2. Describe your dream house.
3. How expensive is housing in your country?

After that, they will ask you to provide some photo identification, such as a driver's license or a passport. They will also ask you for a list of past addresses in order to ensure that your renting history is good. If you were evicted from a previous rental property for any reason, you most likely will be denied a lease.

The next thing owners might ask you for is a recent tax return. They want to know that you earn enough money each year to afford the monthly rent. The last three pieces of information they will probably ask for are your banking information, reference letters from previous landlords, and proof of residency in the country. Proof of residency shows them that you are in the United States legally and will not break the lease.

Track 52

A   If you want to buy a condo or a house in the United States, it is best to contact a real estate agent, or realtor. A realtor's job is to match you with the perfect home—one that is the right size and affordable for you. Realtors get paid when you actually purchase the home, so you have to be careful when dealing with them. Never let a realtor push you into a home you are not sure about. This is a conversation between a realtor and a couple looking to buy a house. Listen and practice the conversation with a partner.

Alice is showing Justin and his wife a home in Denver, Colorado.

Alice   Are you ready to see the inside of the home?

Justin   Yes, we're very excited.

Alice   Let's start with the living room.

Justin   Okay.

Alice   As you can see, there are large bay windows in the living room, and just look at this view.

Justin   It's beautiful.

Alice   This is probably one of the best views in Denver. You can see the white peaks of the Rocky Mountains from here.

Justin   I love it.

Alice   And it's really spacious. You could put a large sofa here and your television on that wall over there, and there's still enough space for an armchair or two.

Justin   Where's the kitchen?

Alice   If we head into the next room, you'll see a large kitchen with a beautiful island table.

Justin   Are there drawers in the island for pots and pans?

Alice   Yes, there are.

⊘ **Words to Know**   bay window   spacious   island table

B   Practice the conversation with a partner. Use the information in the box below.

A   Let's start with the ¹ ....

B   Okay.

A   As you can see, there is ² ....

B   It's ³ ....

1	2	3
bedroom	a high ceiling	nice
bathroom	a new shower	perfect
study	a fireplace	stunning

Language Focus

A There are a number of household items that are common in homes in the United States. Look at the picture of the house and the list of household items.

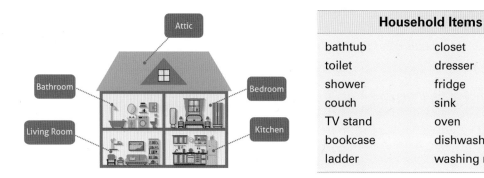

Household Items	
bathtub	closet
toilet	dresser
shower	fridge
couch	sink
TV stand	oven
bookcase	dishwasher
ladder	washing machine

B Match the words in the box to the correct items in the house.

ⓐ toilet   ⓑ bookcase   ⓒ closet   ⓓ couch   ⓔ dresser   ⓕ fridge   ⓖ shower   ⓗ oven

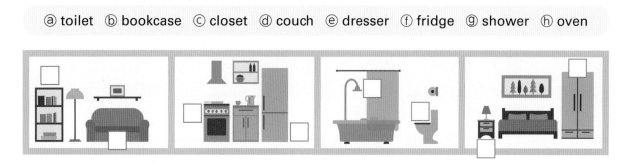

Speak Out | Pair Work

Find a partner. Then, describe your bedroom to him or her. Let your partner draw your bedroom based on your description. Tell him or her what kinds of items you have in your room and where they are located.

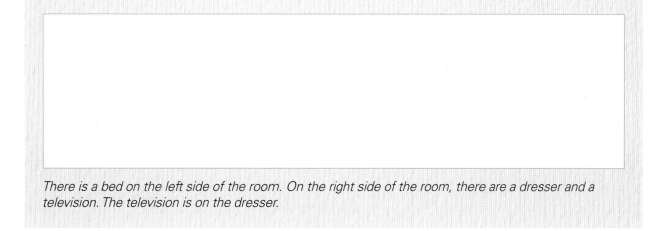

There is a bed on the left side of the room. On the right side of the room, there are a dresser and a television. The television is on the dresser.

Conversation ❷ *Searching for an Apartment*

Track 53

A When looking for an apartment in the United States, you should start your search by looking for available apartments in the classifieds section of the newspaper and on online apartment rental websites. You should also ask friends, and even coworkers, if they are looking for roommates or know anyone who is. Listen and practice the conversation with a partner.

Fran and Kyunghee are talking about finding an apartment.

Fran	Hey, Kyunghee. How's the apartment search going?
Kyunghee	Not well.
Fran	I'm sorry to hear that.
Kyunghee	I found three available apartments online and one in the newspaper, but when I called to ask if they were available, the owners said they had already been rented.
Fran	Apartments are really tough to find in Los Angeles. Where are you staying now?
Kyunghee	I'm staying at my aunt and uncle's house in Santa Monica, but their place is fairly small. I'm sleeping on an air mattress in my baby cousin's bedroom.
Fran	You know what? I might be able to help you.
Kyunghee	How so?
Fran	My roommate's sister is looking for a roommate.
Kyunghee	Really? Where does she live?
Fran	She's renting a place in Los Feliz, but she needs a roommate in order to split the cost of rent.
Kyunghee	I'd love to meet her.
Fran	I'll call my roommate, so the two of you can meet. If you hit it off, you will have found yourself a place!

⊘ Words to Know   rent   fairly   hit it off

B Practice the conversation with a partner. Use the information in the box below.

A My ¹ _____ is looking for a roommate.

B Really? Where does she live?

A She's renting a place ² _____ , but she needs a roommate in order to ³ _____ the cost of rent.

B I'd love to ⁴ _____ .

1	2	3	4
friend	downtown	share	meet her
sister	in the suburbs	divide	make her acquaintance
friend's sister	in the city	split	be introduced to her

Language Focus

A In English, we use the past perfect tense in order to discuss an event which happened at an earlier time than another event in the past. If we use *before* or *after* in the sentence, we use the past simple tense. Look at the examples in the chart.

Past Perfect Tense	Past Simple Tense with *before* or *after*
When I called the owner, she told me the apartment **had** already **been** rented.	I lived in an apartment **before** I decided to buy a house.
I didn't call him until he **had calmed** down.	Judy called Ben **after** she got home from work.
When everyone **had finished** their main courses, the waitress brought them dessert.	Where did you live **before** you moved here?
	What did you do **after** you watched the game?

B Fill in the blanks by using the past perfect tense or the past simple tense.

1. When Jack arrived home, his family _____ (eat) dinner already.

2. I _____ (know) about the situation for a while when Joe finally told me about it.

3. I _____ (live) with my parents before I moved into my own apartment.

4. They went to the sauna after they _____ (be) in the swimming pool.

5. She waited until all the guests _____ (leave).

6. Where did you go before you _____ (arrive) at work today?

Speak Out

Use the timeline below to write about all of the places you have lived in your life. Then, make sentences by using *before* and *after* to tell a classmate about the places.

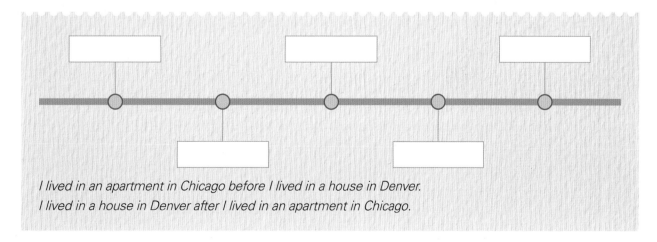

I lived in an apartment in Chicago before I lived in a house in Denver.
I lived in a house in Denver after I lived in an apartment in Chicago.

Conversation ③ *Signing a Lease*

Track 54

A In the United States, the deposit for an apartment or a house usually consists of an amount equal to the first and last months' rent. By law, owners cannot ask you to pay more of a deposit than that amount. How much is a deposit for an apartment or house in your country? Listen and practice the conversation with a partner.

A tenant, Julio, is signing a lease with his landlord, Diane.

Diane Let's go over the details of the lease one more time.

Julio Great. Thanks!

Diane You are going to give me the first and last months' rent as a deposit right now.

Julio Yes, that's right.

Diane And that'll be $1,800.

Julio Correct.

Diane You are also going to give me an amount equal to the first month's rent right now.

Julio Yes. I'm going to give you $1,800 as a deposit and $900 for the first month's rent. The total is $2,700.

Diane Do you have the money with you?

Julio I'll transfer it into your account right now.

Diane Great. Rent is due on the first of the month, so your next rental payment is due on May 1.

Julio Today is the 15th of April, so my next rental payment is due in two weeks?

Diane Yes, that's right. However, your final rental payment will only be $450 because you'll be leaving on the 15th.

Julio Okay, I see.

Diane All right then. Just sign here, and I'll give you the keys to your place.

✓ **Words to Know**   tenant   lease   deposit   transfer

B Practice the conversation with a partner. Use the information in the box below.

A Do you have the money with you?

B I'll ¹_____ it into your account right now.

A Great. Rent is due on the first of the month, so your next ²_____ is due on May 1.

B Today is the 15th, so my next rental payment is due ³_____ ?

1	2	3
wire	rent check	two weeks later
put	payment	two weeks from now
transfer	rental payment	the week after next

Language Focus

During your search for a rental house or apartment, you will find some very strange abbreviations that may be difficult to understand. When people post an advertisement in a newspaper's classified's page, they must pay for each letter, so they often use abbreviations in order to save money. Look at the advertisements below. Then, match the words in the box to their correct abbreviations.

ⓐ bathroom ⓑ bedroom ⓒ finished ⓓ parking ⓔ basement
ⓕ renovated ⓖ apartment ⓗ bungalow ⓘ available ⓙ month

Houses & Apartments

For Rent

Shoreview, MN.

Arizona Ave: 1 bdrm, 1 bath, apt, $500/mo
☐ ☐

Brock Blvd: 3 bdrm, 2 bath, bung + fin bsmt, $1,200/mo
☐ ☐

Canton Dr: 2 bdrm, 1 ½ bath, apt, prkg avail, $650/mo
☐ ☐ ☐

5th Ave: 3 bdrm, 3 bath, bung, big lot, prkg, ren bsmt, $1,400/mo
☐ ☐

Sandra Ln: 2 bdrm, 1 bath, bung, fin bsmt, prkg, garage, $760/mo
☐ ☐

* ½ bath means there is a bathroom with a toilet and a sink but no bathtub or shower.

Speak Out | Pair Work

Imagine that you work at a newspaper and your job is to write advertisements in the classifieds section of the newspaper. Your partner wants to list his or her apartment or house for rent in your newspaper. Ask your partner to describe his or her home to you. Then, write an ad for the home in the space below. Save your partner some money by using the abbreviations above. When you are finished writing your partner's ad, switch roles.

CLASSIFIEDS	
Houses & Apartments For Rent	

Wrap It Up

Vocabulary Check Match the words with their correct definitions.

1. spacious •

   • ⓐ a contractual rental agreement for an apartment or house

2. tenant •

   • ⓑ to get along with someone really well immediately

3. deposit •

   • ⓒ large in size; expansive; roomy

4. lease •

   • ⓓ a person who lives in an apartment or a house which is rented from a landlord

5. hit it off •

   • ⓔ money that is given to the owner of a property while it is being rented but is returned when the terms of the lease have been met

Situation Talk Role-play the following situations with a partner.

Role-Play 1

You are talking to B, your coworker, about your apartment search.

1. Greet B.
2. Tell B it is not going well. Tell B that you found two apartments available online, but when you called the owners, the apartments had already been rented.
3. Tell B that you are definitely interested.
4. Thank B.

Your coworker, A, is looking for an apartment in your city.

1. Greet A. Ask A how the apartment search is going.
2. Say that's too bad. Tell A that your sister's roommate has just moved out and that she is looking for a new roommate. Ask A if he or she is interested in living with a roommate.
3. Tell A that you will arrange a meeting between him or her and your sister.

Role-Play 2

You are the owner of an apartment which is being rented by B.

1. Ask B if you can go over the lease one more time.
2. Tell B that there is a deposit of an amount equal to the first and last months' rent. Tell B that the total is $2,000.
3. Tell B that you also need the first month's rent right now.
4. Say "Great." Tell B to sign the lease.

You are renting an apartment from A.

1. Say yes.
2. Tell A that a $2,000 deposit is fine.
3. Say "Okay." Tell A that you will transfer $3,000 to his or her bank account right now.

Home Rental Scams

Track 55

When renting a house or an apartment, you must watch out for rental scams. Because you are eager and excited to find a place, you are especially vulnerable to these kinds of scams. Do not blindly trust the classifieds or online sites. Make sure that the person you are paying money to actually owns the property. A rental scam occurs when a person receives money from a tenant but does not actually own the property that is being rented. The scammer could be the previous tenant who is trying to steal some money before leaving the apartment. It could also be that the apartment or house does not exist at all. Either way, you are paying someone for a house or an apartment that the person has no legal authority to rent. Here are a few signs that you may be part of a rental scam:

1. The landlord is too eager or excited to lease the apartment. If upon meeting the landlord, you get the feeling that you are being pushed and prodded into signing the lease, you may be the victim of a rental scam. Honest landlords will not act like salespeople. An honest landlord will give you all the information you need about the place but will not be pushy about it.

2. Lots of up-front fees and payments. When you are looking at an apartment, it should be free of charge. If someone is trying to extract a fee from you just to look at an apartment, then you are probably part of a rental scam. Once you have seen the place and want to rent it, you may be asked to pay other strange fees like signing fees or open house fees. These are not real fees. In these cases, you are probably part of a scam. The appropriate payments are a deposit that equals the first and last months' rent, the first month's rent, and perhaps a deposit for the key and a monthly management fee. These are normal fees that go along with renting an apartment or a house.

3. No Lease Necessary. If you are told you do not need a lease, it is quite possible that you are part of a rental scam. A lease not only protects you, but it also protects the owner of the property. An owner who does not want a lease is probably not the actual owner of the property.

Read the article. Check T for true or F for false.
1. A rental scam occurs when a person tries to lease a property he or she does not own. T ☐ / F ☐
2. Looking at an apartment should not cost you any money. T ☐ / F ☐
3. An owner who does not want a lease is probably the actual owner of the property. T ☐ / F ☐

Spaces for Everyone

Public Spaces vs. Private Spaces

When we think about public spaces, we often think about public and private places where all members of society are invited as long as they follow the laws. There is, however, a narrower definition of a public space: a place in a city which is not privately owned but is publicly owned. Unlike coffee shops or fast-food restaurants, these places are paid for and maintained with taxpayers' money. These spaces include local parks, national parks, public schools, and libraries. These spaces are open to the public and are free for residents to enjoy as long as people follow the laws. Over time, the number of publicly owned spaces has decreased.

Discuss the following questions.

1. What kinds of public spaces are common in your country?
2. Which public space do you spend the most time at: the park, the library, school, etc.?
3. Do you wish your city had more public spaces?

Long ago, there were public squares, places where residents in a city would congregate to talk, to share ideas, and to learn about what is happening in their respective cities. People were engaged in local politics and interested in the decisions the local politicians made. These residents also made sure the decisions made by politicians were in the best interests of the public and not a small group of politicians and the politicians' friends.

With the decrease in the number of public spaces, private companies have filled the void with more private spaces such as coffee shops. And everyone is invited as long as they can afford $6.00 lattes and cappuccinos. Let's hope Americans can hold on to the public spaces they have left and not leave them in the hands of private owners.

Conversation ① *Borrowing a Book from the Library*

A Public libraries are great places to visit if you do not have a lot of money to spend on books, CDs, and DVDs. You can borrow them free of charge, and if you return them before their due dates, you do not have to pay anything. Libraries also have Internet connections, so you can use public libraries to check and send emails. What kinds of services are provided at public libraries in your country? Listen and practice the conversation with a partner.

Carlos is visiting his local library. He is looking for a specific book.

Carlos Hi. I'd like to borrow a book, but I'm not from the United States.

Librarian That's okay. Are you here on a student visa?

Carlos Actually, I'm here on a one-year work visa.

Librarian That's fine. Do you have a picture ID?

Carlos I have an American credit card. Will that do?

Librarian I'm sorry, but it has to be a picture ID.

Carlos I have my passport.

Librarian Perfect. Why don't you look for some books to check out? By the time you have found a few, your card will be ready.

Carlos I'm actually looking for a specific book. Do you have *A People's History of the United States* by Howard Zinn?

Librarian Let's see. Z-I-N-N. You're in luck. There is a copy in our stack section. The call number is H29348.

Carlos Thank you so much for your help. I'll be back in a jiffy.

Librarian Don't be too quick. I still have to make your card.

⊘ **Words to Know**   work visa   check out   stack   call number

B Practice the conversation with a partner. Use the information in the box below.

A I'm actually looking for a specific book. Do you have ¹_____ by ²_____?

B You're in luck. There is a copy in our nonfiction section. The call number is B30402.

A Thank you so much for your help. I'll be back in a ³_____.

B Don't be too quick. I still have to make your card.

1	2	3
Blink	Malcolm Gladwell	flash
In Cold Blood	Truman Capote	sec
Syntactic Structures	Noam Chomsky	moment

122 · BIG POT 2

Language Focus

A Libraries are not just about books anymore. Libraries are technological information centers where you can search the Internet, rent movies, and download important documents. Whereas libraries used to be known for their quiet, stale atmospheres, they are now dynamic learning centers. Look at some of the different sections in the library.

Sections of the library	
Internet Section	Periodical Section
Reference Section	Back Volume Section
Study Room Section	Stack Section

B Match the section name with the correct definition by writing the section names in the blanks.

1. _____ : You can find journals, magazines, and newspapers.

2. _____ : You can find documents such as encyclopedias, dictionaries, almanacs, handbooks, directories, reports, bibliographies, indexes, biographies, atlases, and maps.

3. _____ : This is where all of the books are kept.

4. _____ : You can quietly read a book here. It is usually located near the stack section.

5. _____ : You can access the Internet as well as the library's e-collections such as e-databases, e-journals, and e-books.

6. _____ : This is where older volumes of newspapers, periodicals, and magazines are stored.

Speak Out | Pair Work

Find a partner. Then, imagine your partner is a librarian. Based on the comments below, see if your partner can direct you to the correct sections of the library. Write your partner's answers in the blanks. Take turns being the visitor and the librarian.

	Title/Description	Section
1	Where can I find *The DaVinci Code* by Dan Brown?	Stack Section
2	I'm looking for a *New York Times* article from May 24, 2016.	
3	Is there a quiet place I can read in the library?	
4	I'm looking for this month's issue of *Popular Mechanics*.	
5	I'd like to borrow a Spanish-English dictionary.	
6	Where can I send an email to my family back in Korea?	

Conversation ② *Hiking in Yosemite*

A There are a lot of wonderful national parks in the United States which are free for the public to use. This land is preserved for its natural beauty and is not for sale to private citizens and corporations. Millions of Americans and people around the world visit the country's national parks every year. Listen and practice the conversation with a partner.

Nathan and Esther are going to hike in Yosemite National Park.

Nathan Let's check our packs before we go.

Esther Okay. How long is this hike by the way?

Nathan I think the entire trail takes about three hours to complete. It's 8:00 a.m. now, so we'll be back around 11:00 a.m.

Esther Can we grab lunch at the hotel restaurant when we get back?

Nathan That's what I was thinking.

Esther I put some trail mix and some energy bars in my pack in case we get hungry.

Nathan Great. And remember that we can't leave trash on the trail. We have to bring it with us.

Esther Got it.

Nathan How's your water situation?

Esther I know I took a bottle out of the mini-fridge. Oh, no! I forgot it at the hotel. Should I go back and get it?

Nathan We can't go back now. It's getting late. Anyway, I have two bottles of Powerade in my pack. That should be enough for a three-hour trek.

Esther Thanks. I think that's everything then. Are you ready to go?

Nathan One last thing: if you see a bear, keep your distance and don't panic.

Esther Bears?

⊘**Words to Know**   pack   trek   keep one's distance   panic

B Practice the conversation with a partner. Use the information in the box below.

A How's your water situation?

B I know I took a ¹ _____ out of the mini-fridge. Oh, no! I forgot it at the hotel.

A Anyway, I have some in my ² _____ . That should be enough for a three-hour ³ _____ .

1	2	3
can	bag	hike
canteen	rucksack	walk
jug	knapsack	journey

Language Focus

A American English speakers often replace the modal auxiliary verb *mustn't* with *can't*. Although *can't* often relates to inability, it can also be used to talk about prohibition. Look at the examples in the chart.

Inability	Prohibition
I **can't** walk because I'm so hungry.	We **can't** leave trash on the trail.
≠ I must not walk because I'm so hungry.	= We **mustn't** leave trash on the trail.
We **can't** reach the peak. It's too far.	We **can't** park here. It's private.
≠ We mustn't reach the peak. It's too far.	= We **must not** park here. It's private.

B Check "I" if *can't* in the sentences relates to inability or "P" if *can't* relates to prohibition.

1. I **can't** see the mountain peak. Let's hike a bit farther. I ☐ P ☐

2. You **can't** bring your pets here. It's a pet-free zone. I ☐ P ☐

3. John **can't** call his parents. There's no signal at the campsite. I ☐ P ☐

4. I **can't** bring another bottle of water. My pack is already too heavy. I ☐ P ☐

5. They **can't** set their tents up in this area. There are too many bears. I ☐ P ☐

6. You **can't** feed the wildlife. Human food may cause serious health problems. I ☐ P ☐

Speak Out | Group Work

Make a group of five students. Now, imagine you are the owners of a popular campsite in your country. Write down the five most important things visitors can't or mustn't do at your campsite. Then, give a reason for making the rule. Share your group's campsite rules with the class.

Campsite Rules

1 _____
2 _____
3 _____
4 _____
5 _____

Conversation ③ *A Summer Block Party*

Track 59

A A lot of neighborhoods in the United States have block parties during the summer. A block party occurs when one or more blocks are closed off to traffic, and residents of that neighborhood throw a party. Tables are set up on the street where food and drinks are made available for residents to enjoy. At block parties, people enjoy socializing, playing games, and listening to music. Listen and practice the conversation with a partner.

Shinhye is attending a block party with her friend, Robert.

Robert	Is this your first block party?
Shinhye	Yes, it is.
Robert	You're going to love it!
Shinhye	I'm a little nervous because I don't really know what to do. I mean, is all of this food free?
Robert	Yup! It's a potluck. Because we brought chips, soda, and hot dogs, we get to eat whatever we want.
Shinhye	Everyone shares with one another?
Robert	Right. All attendees bring a few dishes, and then they share what they've brought.
Shinhye	We don't really have block parties in Korea.
Robert	Why not?
Shinhye	Most people live in apartments. But we do have parties with our neighbors on the rooftops of our apartment buildings.
Robert	That's exactly what this is. It's a way to get to know your neighbors better.
Shinhye	I'm starving. Do we have to wait until the older folks have had their food first?
Robert	Nope. Just grab a plate and work your way from that end of the table to the other end.

⊘ **Words to Know**   potluck   attendee   rooftop   older folks

B Practice the conversation with a partner. Use the information in the box below.

A   Is all of this food ¹ _____ ?

B   It's a potluck. Because we brought chips, soda, and ² _____ , we get to eat whatever we want.

A   Everyone shares with one another?

B   Right. ³ _____ bring a few dishes, and then they share what they've brought.

1	2	3
for us	hamburgers	All of the participants
okay to eat	tacos	All who attend
free of charge	pasta salad	Residents in attendance

Language Focus

A When everyone at a party brings one, two, or three items for everyone to enjoy, it is called a potluck party. Look at the chart about common food items for potlucks.

Parts of a Potluck Dinner				
Soup / Stew	**Salad**	**Main Courses**	**Desserts**	**Drinks**
chili	garden salad	hamburgers	cake	soda
potato soup	potato salad	hotdogs	brownies	beer
broccoli soup	pasta salad	bratwursts	rice krispy treats	spirits
chicken soup	coleslaw	tacos	watermelon	lemonade
beef stroganoff	corn salad	steak / pork ribs	grapes	juice

B Fill in the dialogue with three of your own food items. You do not have to choose items from the chart. Then, practice it with a partner.

A Are you going to the potluck block party?

B Of course.

A What are you brining?

B I'm bringing chili, coleslaw, and watermelon. How about you?

A I'm bringing _____ , _____ , and
_____ .

Speak Out | Group Work

Make a group of five students. Then, imagine the five of you are having a potluck party. Write down your group members' food and drink items in the chart. When everyone has shared information about their items, fill your paper plate below with four items and a drink from your group's potluck items. Which dishes and drinks did you decide to try? Which food and drink items were the most popular?

Name	Food Item 1	Food Item 2	Drink

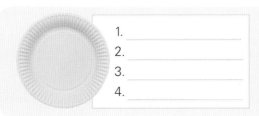

1. _____
2. _____
3. _____
4. _____

Wrap It Up

Fill in the blanks with the correct answers.

1. There were a bunch of people at the _____ last weekend.
   ⓐ folks ⓑ potluck

2. Let's check our _____ before we leave. This is an eight-hour hike, and I don't want to forget anything.
   ⓐ distance ⓑ packs

3. You can _____ books for free from public libraries. ⓐ check out ⓑ call number

4. That was quite a _____. My feet are killing me! ⓐ stack ⓑ trek

5. All _____ must pay $35 to participate in this event. ⓐ attendees ⓑ rooftops

Situation Talk

A **Role-play the following situation with a partner.**

Role **A**	Role **B**
You want to borrow a book from the public library.	*You are a librarian at the public library.*
1. Tell B that you would like to check out a book, but you are not from the United States.	1. Tell A that that is not a problem. Ask A if he or she has a picture ID.
2. Tell B that you have a passport.	2. Tell A that a passport will work just fine.
3. Ask B if the library has *Harry Potter and the Chamber of Secrets.*	3. Tell A that that book's call number is J39400. Tell A that he or she should find the book and that by the time he or she returns, his or her card will be ready.
4. Tell B that that sounds like a good idea. Thank B for his or her help.	

B **Find a partner. Then, plan a five-day camping trip to a national park in the United States or your home country. You can use the Internet in order to research national parks and fees associated with campsites. Complete the chart below with information about your camping trip. When you are finished, present your trip information to the class.**

Number of Days	National Park Location	Campsite Fee Per Night	Activities You Plan to Do	Food and Drink You Plan to Bring
5				

We plan to visit Seoraksan National Park in Korea. Campsite fees are about $35 per night …

Go to the Park

Track 60

Nowadays, too many public parks in the United States, especially in the suburbs, remain empty or very lightly used by the public. In the past, picnickers could be found staking out the best shaded spots in public parks all across the United States on Saturdays and Sundays. These days, it is not uncommon to drive by a public park and to see no more than five people enjoying the park and its amenities. There are several reasons why public parks remain lightly or completely unused by local residents.

First of all, Americans are far less active than they were just a generation or two ago. Part of this can be attributed to the advent of the Internet, video games, and more sophisticated home entertainment systems. Why go to the park when you can stay home in an air-conditioned house or apartment and play video games with your friends via the Internet? If you become bored with playing games, you can always transition to the sofa for just about any movie of your choice. Between Netflix, Amazon, YouTube, and cable television, you are sure to find something entertaining to watch. Want a snack? Shuffle your way over to the kitchen for a bag of potato chips and a refreshing soda. And if games and movies do not interest you, there are countless music streaming services available, so you can listen to just about any song ever recorded in human history.

What these activities do not offer is physical movement, which is so important for our heart health. In the past, picnickers brought frisbees and American footballs to the park to toss around for fun. These activities required movement, which in turn burned calories and kept people thinner and healthier. In this new age, we need to look to the past for some solutions to our current health crises. A lot of our problems stem from the way we are living. Why not pick one weekend a month to unplug, pack up a picnic basket, go into the garage and find that old frisbee or football, and enjoy the park the way our parents did when they were young?

Read the article. Answer these questions.
1. According to the article, why do public parks remain unused by local residents nowadays?
2. How did past generations enjoy parks?
3. What advice does the writer give to the current generation?

Answer Key

Unit 01 Fashion and Style

Conversation ❶ Language Focus B   p.13

(Answers may vary.)
1. Jenny is thinking about getting a pair of blue jeans.
2. Jenny is considering taking a trip.
3. Jenny is contemplating going to graduate school.
4. Jenny is thinking about moving to a new house.
5. Jenny is considering buying a pair of high heels.

Conversation ❷ Language Focus A   p.15

f, c, b, e, d, a

Language Focus B
1. let the cat out of the bag
2. under the weather
3. see eye to eye
4. a piece of cake
5. the best of both worlds
6. you can't judge a book by its cover

Conversation ❸ Language Focus B   p.17

1. g	**2.** b	**3.** a
4. e	**5.** d	**6.** f
7. c	**8.** h	

Wrap It Up Vocabulary Check   p.18

1. intimidating	2. unique
3. piercing	4. hoodies
5. judge	

Just So You Know   p.19

1. F	2. T	3. F

Unit 02 Sports Nuts

Conversation ❶ Language Focus B   p.23

1. Midwest	2. Southwest
3. West	4. Northeast
5. Southeast	

Conversation ❷ Language Focus B   p.25

1. dribbled	2. hit
3. threw	4. kicked
5. spiked	6. caught

Conversation ❸ Language Focus B   p.27

1. Jiwoo is 5 feet 8 inches tall.
2. Byunghun's house is 6.214 miles from here.
3. An American football field is 91.44 meters long.
4. Charles is 7 feet 2 inches tall.

Wrap It Up Vocabulary Check   p.28

1. ⓒ	2. ⓔ	3. ⓑ
4. ⓐ	5. ⓓ	

Just So You Know   p.29

1. Americans settled the West together. / American men fought together in World War II.
2. Team sports organizations were created so that young people could learn how to work together at young ages.
3. Team sports are also meant for the fans of the sports.

Unit 03 Americans and Their Cars

Conversation ❶ Language Focus B   p.33

1. NIV	2. IV	3. NIV
4. NIV	5. NIV	6. IV

Conversation ❷ Language Focus B   p.35

1. up	2. out	3. on
4. up	5. over	6. off
7. off		

Wrap It Up Vocabulary Check   p.38

1. ⓑ	2. ⓐ	3. ⓑ
4. ⓐ	5. ⓑ	

Just So You Know   p.39

1. T	2. F	3. T

Unit 04 Guns in America

Conversation ❶ Language Focus B   p.43

(Answers may vary.)
1. Would you like
2. Do you want

3. Are you interested

4. What do you think

Conversation ❷ Language Focus B   p.45

(Answers may vary.)

1. scared, Can we leave?

2. nervous, I'd like to get out of here.

3. uncomfortable, Can we take off?

4. disgusted, I'd like to go somewhere else.

Speak Out

(Answers may vary.)

The dog makes me really uncomfortable. Can we take off?

The man with the gun is making me nervous. I'd like to go somewhere else.

The man who is smoking makes me feel annoyed. Can we leave?

The haunted house is making me feel scared. I'd like to get out of here.

Conversation ❸ Language Focus B   p.47

1. underground	**2.** French fries
3. apartment	**4.** rubber
5. sweets	**6.** rubbish
7. elevator	**8.** cab
9. trolley	**10.** bar

Speak Out

Put the luggage in the trunk of the car.

She drives a truck professionally.

Would you like a cookie?

They parked in the parking lot.

Where can I find a gas station?

Wrap It Up Vocabulary Check   p.48

1. population	**2.** plainclothes
3. civilians	**4.** dormitory
5. firearm	

Just So You Know   p.49

1. Gun violence is one of the most troubling aspects of American culture.

2. The United States has an amendment in its constitution that gives citizens the right to own guns.

3. There are approximately 39,000 gun deaths per year.

Unit **05** **Dating**

Conversation ❶ Language Focus B   p.53

(Answers may vary.)

1. ① You have a nice beard.

  ② You look great in that suit.

  ③ I like your hairstyle.

2. ① You have beautiful eyes.

  ② Your dress looks really nice.

  ③ I adore your handbag.

Conversation ❷ Language Focus B   p.55

1. busy	**2.** Unfortunately
3. free	**4.** meeting
5. doing	**6.** meet
7. then	

Speak Out

(Answers may vary.)

A Are you busy on Friday, Andi?

B No, I'm not. I'm free on Friday.

A Brian, do you have any plans on Saturday?

B Unfortunately, I have plans on Saturday.

A Are you doing anything tonight, Chris?

B No, I'm free tonight.

A Shania, are you busy this Saturday?

B I'm sorry, but I'm busy on Saturday.

Conversation ❸ Language Focus B   p.57

1. Is there anyone here

2. Are you

Wrap It Up Vocabulary Check   p.58

1. ⓒ	**2.** ⓔ	**3.** ⓐ
4. ⓓ	**5.** ⓑ	

Just So You Know   p.59

1. F	**2.** F	**3.** T

Unit **06** **Travel in America**

Conversation ❶ Language Focus   p.63

1. ⓖ	**2.** ⓑ	**3.** ⓕ
4. ⓓ	**5.** ⓔ	**6.** ⓐ
7. ⓒ		

Conversation ❷ Language Focus B   p.65

1. ⓑ	**2.** ⓐ	**3.** ⓔ
4. ⓕ	**5.** ⓒ	**6.** ⓓ

Conversation ❸ Language Focus B   p.67

1. ETA	**2.** AKA	**3.** FYI
4. TBA	**5.** ATM	**6.** DIY
7. RSVP	**8.** TGIF	

Wrap It Up Vocabulary Check   p.68

1. ⓐ	**2.** ⓑ	**3.** ⓐ
4. ⓑ	**5.** ⓑ	

Just So You Know p.69

1. A staycation is when you take days off from work but stay at home or in your city.
2. They are busy with work or home life.
3. The purpose of a vacation is to unwind and recharge your batteries.

Unit 07 Health Care

Conversation ❶ Language Focus B p.73

(Answers may vary.)
1. You should take some aspirin.
2. Why don't you put a pain relief patch on your back?
3. You'd better use the aloe vera gel.
4. If I were you, I would go to the ER immediately.

Conversation ❷ Language Focus B p.75

1. Is, okay, be perfect
2. available, afraid, good
3. unable, reschedule
4. opening, works

Conversation ❸ Language Focus p.77

1. ⓔ 　　2. ⓒ 　　3. ⓕ
4. ⓓ 　　5. ⓑ 　　6. ⓐ

Wrap It Up Vocabulary Check p.78

1. diagnosed 　　2. cancellation
3. hoarse 　　4. sprained
5. opening

Just So You Know p.79

1. F 　　2. T 　　3. T

Unit 08 At the Hair Salon

Conversation ❶ Language Focus B p.83

1. ⓓ 　　2. ⓒ 　　3. ⓑ
4. ⓕ 　　5. ⓔ 　　6. ⓐ

Conversation ❷ Language Focus B p.85

1. colored 　　2. shaved
3. curly perm 　　4. bangs

Conversation ❸ Language Focus p.87

1. pedicure 　　2. aromatherapy
3. waxing 　　4. massage
5. facial 　　6. manicure

Wrap It Up Vocabulary Check p.88

1. ⓐ 　　2. ⓓ 　　3. ⓑ
4. ⓔ 　　5. ⓒ

Just So You Know p.89

1. They were dentists and surgeons.
2. Bloodletting was a common procedure which is not practiced today.
3. The red represents blood, and the white represents the white cloth which covers the wound.

Unit 09 Professional Life

Conversation ❶ Language Focus B p.93

1. Type A 　　2. Type B 　　3. Type B
4. Type A 　　5. Type A 　　6. Type B

Conversation ❷ Language Focus p.95

1. ⓘ 　　2. ⓕ 　　3. ⓐ
4. ⓖ 　　5. ⓓ 　　6. ⓒ
7. ⓗ 　　8. ⓑ 　　9. ⓔ

Conversation ❸ Language Focus B p.97

/d/: achieved, stayed, earned, used
/t/: asked, washed, typed, worked
/ɪd/: appreciated, created, visited, provided

Wrap It Up Vocabulary Check p.98

1. ⓑ 　　2. ⓐ 　　3. ⓐ
4. ⓑ 　　5. ⓐ

Just So You Know p.99

1. F 　　2. T 　　3. F

Unit 10 Weddings

Conversation ❶ Language Focus B p.103

1. N 　　2. F 　　3. F
4. N 　　5. N 　　6. F

Conversation ❷ Language Focus p.105

1. espresso machine 　　2. bed linen
3. microwave 　　4. dinnerware
5. blender 　　6. pots and pans
7. iron 　　8. vacuum cleaner

Conversation ❸ Language Focus B p.107

(Answers may vary.)

1. I was thinking that I would wear a tuxedo.
2. I was thinking of wearing a red dress.
3. I was thinking about requesting an exciting song.
4. I was thinking of eating chicken.
5. I was thinking that I would dance with you.
6. I was thinking about drinking a cocktail.
7. I was thinking that I would spend the night at the hotel.

Wrap It Up Vocabulary Check   p.108

1. reception   2. propose
3. open bar   4. awful
5. electrifying

Just So You Know   p.109

1. A growing number of couples are having do-it-yourself wedding ceremonies.
2. Friends and family members pitch in with decorations, a cake, food, and photographs.
3. The groom should respect the bride's wishes and try to give her the wedding of her dreams.

Unit 11 | Finding a Home

Conversation ❶ Language Focus B   p.113

ⓑ, ⓓ, ⓗ, ⓕ, ⓖ, ⓐ, ⓔ, ⓒ

Conversation ❷ Language Focus B   p.115

1. had eaten   2. had known
3. lived   4. were
5. had left   6. arrived

Conversation ❸ Language Focus   p.117

ⓖ, ⓙ, ⓑ, ⓒ, ⓓ, ⓘ, ⓗ, ⓕ, ⓐ, ⓔ

Wrap It Up Vocabulary Check   p.118

1. ⓒ   2. ⓓ   3. ⓔ
4. ⓐ   5. ⓑ

Just So You Know   p.119

1. F   2. T   3. F

Unit 12 | Spaces for Everyone

Conversation ❶ Language Focus B   p.123

1. Periodical Section
2. Reference Section
3. Stack Section
4. Study Room Section
5. Internet Section

6. Back Volume Section

Speak Out
1. Stack Section
2. Back Volume Section
3. Study Room Section
4. Periodical Section
5. Reference Section
6. Internet Section

Conversation ❷ Language Focus B   p.125

1. I   2. P   3. I
4. I   5. P   6. P

Conversation ❸ Language Focus B   p.127

(Answers may vary.)
hamburgers, corn salad, soda

Wrap It Up Vocabulary Check   p.128

1. ⓑ   2. ⓑ   3. ⓐ
4. ⓑ   5. ⓐ

Just So You Know   p.129

1. Americans are less active than they used to be, and they have home entertainment systems to keep them busy.
2. They had picnics and played frisbee and football at the park.
3. The writer advises young people to unplug for one weekend a month and go to the park.

memo

memo

memo